The
TEDDY BEAR
HALL OF FAME

ALSO BY MICHÈLE BROWN

Royal Recipes

New Book of First Names

Woman Talk

How to Interview and Be Interviewed

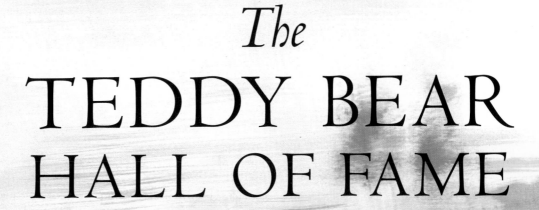

The
TEDDY BEAR
HALL OF FAME

A Century of Historic Bears

PRESENTED BY

The Teddy Bear Museum
STRATFORD-UPON-AVON

Michèle Brown

PHOTOGRAPHS BY

Gerrit Buntrock

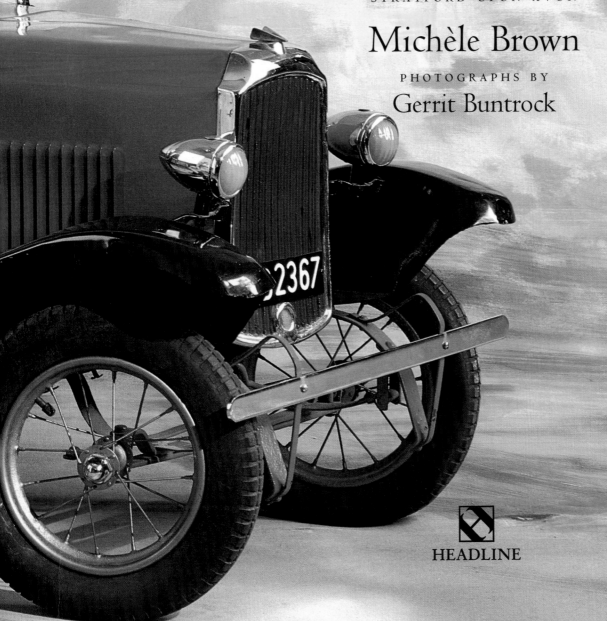

HEADLINE

First published in 1996
by
HEADLINE BOOK PUBLISHING

10 9 8 7 6 5 4 3 2 1

BRITISH LIBRARY CATALOGUING IN PUBLICATION DATA
Brown, Michèle, 1947-
The teddy bear hall of fame: a century of historic bears
1. Teddy bears – History
I. Title
688.7'24'09

ISBN 0 7472 1803 X

Design and art direction by Peter Ward
Typeset by Keyboard Services, Luton, Beds
Printed and bound in Italy by
Canale & C. S.p.A.

HEADLINE BOOK PUBLISHING
A division of Hodder Headline PLC
338 Euston Road
London NW1 3BH

Contents

ACKNOWLEDGEMENTS

My thanks to the following for all their help with *The Teddy Bear Hall of Fame*: Sylvia Coote and the staff of The Teddy Bear Museum (Deborah Bunn, Margaret Smith, Val Perry and Rachel Course) and Ray Coote; Ken Boyden, of the *Stratford Herald*, who donated the 1920s bear seen seated at the foot of page 23, Neil Miller of the Dean's Company, Oliver Holmes, John Parkes and Jackie Revitt of Merrythought, Rosemary and Paul Volpp, Angela Humphrey, Jochen and Jutta Frank, Richard Baker, Pollock's Toy Museum, London and Mark Ellis of The Trading Post, Stratford-upon-Avon.

I should also like to thank the editor, Celia Kent, the designer, Peter Ward and the photographer, Gerrit Buntrock. Their hard work and their commitment to the project have been very much appreciated.

The poem from *Summoned by Bells* by John Betjeman is reproduced by kind permission of John Murray (Publishers) Ltd.

PICTURE ACKNOWLEDGEMENTS

All photographs are by Gerrit Buntrock with the exception of the pictures on the following pages:

Christie's Images 18, 19, 25 26, 42, 50, 54, 58, 70, 93, 101
Jürgen & Marianne Cieslik. Steiff Teddy Bears/Love for a Lifetime 24, 81, 96
Collection Kiok Siem, Photographer Louk Heimans © De Agostini Editions 16, 64
Mary Evans Picture Library 10, 11, 14L, 15
Francis Loney 48, 108, 137, 138
Merrythought 32, 128, 131
The New York Public Library 68
Peter Newark's American Pictures 14R
Smithsonian Institution 52
Teddy Bears of Witney 51
Paul and Rosemary Volpp 80

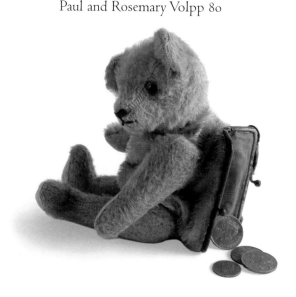

DEDICATION

For Gyles, whose brilliant idea it was.

A
TEDDY
BEAR
HISTORY

When Bears Really Were Bears

Let bears and lions growl and fight,
For 'tis their nature too.

Isaac Watts 1674–1748

Bears when first born are shapeless
masses of white flesh a little larger
than mice, their claws alone being
prominent. The mother then licks them
gradually into proper shape.

Pliny the Elder, *Natural History*, AD 77

Exit, pursued by a bear.

William Shakespeare, *The Winter's Tale* Act III
scene 3, 1611

EVERY YEAR hundreds of thousands of visitors, from every corner of the globe, flock to Stratford-upon-Avon, to visit the places associated with Shakespeare, his family and his life. Many of those who come to pay tribute to the world's greatest writer, at his birthplace in Henley Street, also make their way down the road to the home of William Shakesbeare. At the Museum they enjoy a very different phenomenon, one which was not even dreamed of when Shakespeare walked the streets of Stratford, but which, since the opening years of the twentieth century, has also achieved worldwide fame and admiration — the Teddy Bear.

The Teddy Bear Museum collection is displayed in an oak-beamed Elizabethan building in the heart of Stratford-upon-Avon. The house is first mentioned in a document dated 1563, the year before William Shakespeare was born. Although it has undergone many changes over nearly four centuries, and served many different functions, the building began as part of a farmhouse.

Being a farmhouse, the Museum building would have been no stranger to all sorts of animals — cats, dogs, sheep, mice, cows, pigs, horses, donkeys, frogs and chickens. We can get an idea of how much these animals were an integral part of our ancestors' everyday lives by the fact that they crop up time and time again in the popular verses and nursery rhymes handed down the generations. 'Three Blind Mice', 'Ride a Cock Horse to Banbury Cross', 'Baa Baa Black Sheep', 'A Frog He Would a-Wooing Go', 'Goosey Goosey Gander' are just a few of the titles which are still familiar today. But there are no familiar rhymes about bears because bears were not seen as familiar, comforting domestic creatures. They were huge, fierce, aggressive wild animals.

In the sixteenth century, bears still roamed wild in various parts of

A SIXTEENTH-CENTURY
GERMAN WOODCUT OF A
DANCING BEAR PERFORMING
WITH A GROUP OF MUSICIANS—
NOTICE THE BEAR'S FIERCE
CLAWS.

Europe, but chained and cowed dancing bears were the only bears with which most people would have had any contact. The nineteenth-century passion for scientific knowledge led to the setting up of zoos where bears, like other dangerous wild animals, could be viewed from a safe distance. Unless they were captured and humiliated in this way the general image of bears in the past was threatening and alarming. In Shakespeare's plays a bear is mentioned in *The Winter's Tale*, where it performs the anti-social function of eating several of the characters and gives rise to one of the best-known stage directions ever coined, 'Exit, pursued by a bear.'

ABOVE: TWO NINETEENTH—
CENTURY IMAGES OF
PERFORMING BEARS WITH
STROLLING PLAYERS.

Because of their fierce nature and great strength, bears featured frequently in the heraldic devices of aristocratic European families as potent symbols of their own power. This over-riding perception of bears as powerful and dangerous was held right up until the beginning of the present century.

Throughout the world, not just in Europe, the power and unpredictable nature of bears made them objects of fear and admiration. Their habits, and the myths which grew up around these habits, added a layer of mystique and mystery as well. In winter, bears go into partial hibernation in winter dens and live on their stored fat. But because they appear to live on nothing at all, and because it is during hibernation that the females give birth to the cubs, all sorts of stories grew up about where they went and what happened to them when they were no longer visible. In Siberian Russia, where bears were a familiar part of life, people believed that they went down to the underworld during the winter and were given messages by the spirits of the dead. Bear cubs are very small, less than one kilo, when they are born and from Roman times, and maybe even before that, it was widely believed that they were not born fully formed but had to be licked into shape by their mothers.

The fact that bears can walk on their hind legs, like human beings, led people to imagine they shared other, less easily defined, human characteristics, particularly human intelligence. So in many cultures they were regarded as sources of great natural wisdom. In North America, where black and brown bears roamed wild, native North Americans venerated them, giving them the name of the wisest family member – 'Grandfather'. And it was in North America, at the turn of the century, that bears acquired a completely new name and with it a very different reputation.

EVEN IN THE TWENTIETH
CENTURY (THIS PICTURE IS
FROM A FRENCH MAGAZINE
PUBLISHED IN 1901) THE SIGHT
OF A DANCING BEAR WAS
CONSIDERED AN AMUSING
ENTERTAINMENT.

The Classic Teddy is Born

THE PERIOD FROM 1902 to the outbreak of the First World War in 1914 saw the development of the classic, traditional teddy on both sides of the Atlantic. The bears made during this period are the ones most prized by today's teddy-bear lovers and dealers (not always the same thing!), not just because their rarity attracts high prices but because their style set the standard for the rest of the century.

Teddy bears differ from previous toy bears because the fierce and threatening elements of the wild bears have been taken away. A teddy bear has the lovable characteristics of a doll and the appealing helplessness of a small child. Nineteenth-century bear toys, whether the carved wooden pull-alongs of Russia or the fur-covered automata of France, had retained the menacing nature of the real thing.

America gave the teddy bear its name so it is hardly surprising that the first American teddies are highly collectable. Early American bears had particularly sweet faces, more so than their European counterparts. Ideal Novelty and Toy Company bears of this early period are made of short mohair plush. They have triangular faces with wide-set ears and long snouts. Their bodies are long in comparison with German bears. Their limbs are unnaturally straight and they have distinctive long feet, tapering to quite a sharp point. Like most early bears they are firmly stuffed with wood shavings called wood-wool or excelsior, an American tradename for an especially fine type of wood-wool. One greatly prized early Ideal bear also has 'googly' eyes, and is generally presumed to represent the wide-eyed bear cub in the famous Berryman cartoon of President 'Teddy' Roosevelt.

Ideal was not the only American toy company making bears. By the end of 1906 America was 'bear crazy', and many firms rushed to fill demand. Since no one could have foreseen a time when teddy bears would become prized collectables, it is not surprising that no great care was taken over labelling. It is therefore rarely possible to identify early bears exactly. Identification is based on similarity to examples with a known history made by particular companies. Unless such evidence exists, with photographs for example, attempts at identification are always rather haphazard because many firms copied the early Ideal bears and also copied from each other.

American companies whose pre-1914 bears fetch very high prices today include the American Doll and Toy Manufacturing Company, the Aetna Toy Animal Company, the Bruin Manufacturing Company (BMC), Hecla (whose bears were very like the German bears made by Steiff), the Harman Manufacturing Company and Gund.

In their efforts to beat the competition from imported German teddy bears, American manufacturers experimented with novelty bears. Columbia Teddy Bear Manufacturers, for example, produced 'The Laughing Roosevelt Bear', whose wide toothy grin was supposed to imitate the president's famous smile. The Strauss Manufacturing Company made a 'self-whistling' bear with a device in its tummy which created a whistling sound when the bear was tipped back and forth. Several manufacturers sold 'electric-eye' teddies whose eyes, operated by batteries, lit up when the bear was squeezed. One of the disadvantages of these was that the bear had to be unpicked to replace the battery and then sewn up again!

Americans were also great enthusiasts for dressed bears. But despite all these innovations most of the newly formed American companies were fairly short-lived, like the Bruin Manufacturing Company which only lasted from 1907 to 1909. One notable exception is the Gund Manufacturing Company, which made its first bears in 1906 and is still making them today.

On the other side of the Atlantic, in Germany, there was a long-established toy industry ready and eager to exploit the craze for the new toy. Teddy bears were designed along similar lines to their American counterparts but because they had developed quite separately there were distinct differences. Like the early American bears they were much closer to reality than the cuddly toy bears of later generations. But in Germany this resemblance to real bears was even more marked, and it remained a feature far longer than in other countries.

Classic German bears had humps reminiscent of those of wild bears. Their faces, with long snouts, were closer to nature, albeit without the frightening fangs. The tops of their back legs curved out realistically and their back feet were large and oval shaped. The arms were long enough for the bear to be able to stand on four legs as in real life, while the front paws showed a noticeable curve. From about 1908 growlers became a fairly standard feature, although the noise they made probably sounded more like a sheep than a bear!

A number of German firms from this period made similar, high-quality bears, all of which now fetch extravagant prices in the salerooms. The best known of the original German firms is Steiff, which captured the bulk of the American market and which still leads the field today.

13

HOW THE TEDDY BEAR GOT ITS NAME

One of the reasons for the teddy bear's extraordinary success is undoubtedly the name, which seems to sum up all the cosy characteristics and similarity to humans that make the bear so appealing. There can be few people who do not know that it was named after Theodore Roosevelt, the 26th President of the United States. But if the new toy had been dubbed Theodore Bear, rather than the more familiar and relaxed 'Teddy', his appeal might not have been so great, his success would not have been quite so extraordinary, and the world would have been a sadder and less friendly place.

KEEN SPORTSMAN THEODORE 'TEDDY' ROOSEVELT (ABOVE) ON HIS NORTH DAKOTA RANCH IN 1885, AND (ABOVE RIGHT) AS DEPICTED BY BERRYMAN IN THE CARTOON WHICH GAVE THE TEDDY BEAR HIS NAME.

DRAWING THE LINE IN MISSISSIPPI

On 14 November 1902 President Roosevelt was out hunting near Little Sunflower River in Mississippi. He was relaxing after some hard political bargaining over the disputed boundary between the states of Mississippi and Louisiana. Thinking to please him, his hosts captured and stunned a small black bear cub and tied it to a tree to make an easy target for the President's gun. Far from pleasing the President, they found they had offended him, by implying he would contemplate such an unsporting action as killing a tethered animal. 'Spare the bear!' proclaimed the President in ringing tones.

This early example of public relations worked well for Theodore Roosevelt. The *Washington Star* brought the news to the nation: 'President called after the bear had been lassoed, but he refused to make an unsportsmanlike shot.'

The *Washington Star's* political cartoonist, Clifford K. Berryman, immortalised the moment in a drawing which emphasised the child-like helplessness of the little bear cub and the moral rectitude of Roosevelt. The cartoon also carried the political implication that such an upright president could not be persuaded to make political decisions, such as the drawing of a state line, for the wrong reasons.

The story, and the drawing of the bear cub, struck a chord with millions of people. From that moment, until he retired from public life, President Roosevelt's career was symbolised by 'Teddy's Bear', which Berryman used in all his cartoons and which was a key feature of the President's successful re-election campaign of 1905.

In the United States, the name of the cartoon bear cub was first exploited by a Brooklyn storekeeper called Morris Michtom. He and his wife Rose were Russian immigrants. Rose made soft toys to sell alongside the stationery and confectionery in their shop on Thompson Avenue. When Rose made an appealing bear-cub toy Morris made good use of the current news story by displaying newspaper cuttings and the famous cartoon in the shop window along-side the toy, and giving it the label 'Teddy's Bear'.

The toy bear was an immediate success and the founding of the Michtoms' fortune. By the end of the following year, 1903, with the financial backing of America's largest toy wholesalers, Butler Brothers, they had formed their successful business, The Ideal Novelty and Toy Company.

A HEROIC IMAGE OF THE PRESIDENT USED DURING HIS 1905 RE-ELECTION CAMPAIGN.

Although the bear craze took off almost immediately in the States, the term 'teddy bear' (the 's had been quietly dropped) did not enter the language as the accepted term for a soft toy bear until 1906. In November that year it was first used in print in the trade magazine, *Playthings*, by the distributors E. L. Horsman and Company, to advertise bear mascots for use on the new-fangled horseless carriages. A month later the name 'teddy bear' was used by the same company to advertise toy bears themselves, and from then on it was adopted by toy companies the world over.

ONE OF THE successful new German companies set up specifically to make bears during this period was Schreyer and Co., which was started in 1912. Gebrüder Bing, on the other hand, was already an established toy firm. It developed out of a firm founded in the nineteenth century to make kitchenware and mechanically operated tin toys. In about 1908 Bing began making stylish, quality teddy bears, many of them clearly based on the Steiff pattern. This caused conflict, particularly when Bing started to use a trademark button to identify its bears similar to the established Steiff trademark ear button.

As well as making conventional teddy bears, the company built on its long-standing expertise by specialising in mechanical bears. One of the most successful lines was the somersaulting bear produced in 1910. This again brought them into conflict with Steiff, who argued that it broke one of their patents.

'THE SKATER' – A BING MECHANICAL BEAR SHOWN WITH ITS ORIGINAL KEY.

Famous Bing mechanical bears include the footballer, the skier and both roller-skating and ice-skating bears. A Bing mechanical bear is a very desirable addition to any collection but they are now very expensive. One reason, apart from the delightful craftsmanship, is that in 1932, when so many other teddy-bear firms were enjoying a measure of success, Bing went into receivership and was sold off. The number of Bing bears is therefore strictly limited.

In addition to such well-known and established companies, early bears by lesser known makers, such as Strunz, can be identified. Numerous unidentified new soft-toy firms also flourished in Germany and disappeared relatively quickly.

Britain, in its turn, responded enthusiastically to the bear mania in the United States and Germany. It became the second major customer, after the States, for Steiff bears, many of which were styled specifically for the British market. Incidentally, most of the mohair yarn used to make the plush from which early German bears were styled came from British mills.

Traditionally the first British-made, jointed, plush bear is said to have been the work of J. K. Farnell and Company. This was a London firm established in 1840 to make small fabric articles such as pen wipers. In 1897, the founder's two children turned it into a soft-toy company. Josef Eisenmann, a German-born toy distributor who imported German bears, is said to have suggested that the company make teddy bears when he was unable to bring in enough bears to meet demand. Sadly no one knows where the first Farnell bears are now to be found, because a lack of labelling makes reliable identification of the earliest British bears impossible.

A British company that still makes bears, some ninety years on, is Dean's. Originally a traditional publisher, Dean's developed indestructible rag books for children and changed its name to the Dean's Rag Book Company in 1903. From

THE TEDDY BEAR HALL OF FAME

producing rag books with a teddy-bear theme, in 1907, they went on to make cut-out-and-sew rag teddies in 1908. Like the Farnell company, they were encouraged by teddy-bear importer Josef Eisenmann, who was one of their directors.

Many other smaller British soft-toy firms sprang up at this time. William J. Terry (Terryer Toys) and the British United Toy Manufacturing Company (Omega Toys) were among the best-known names. Nevertheless, despite many delightful American and British bears, the early stages of the teddy bear's history were indisputably dominated by German teddy bears, which set the bench mark for traditional quality and design.

A VERY EARLY BRITISH BEAR GLIMPSED IN THE BACKGROUND OF A DEAN'S SAND TOYS ADVERTISING PROMOTION OF 1917.

SOME TEDDY BEAR MILESTONES

1902 In November Morris and Rose Michtom's new soft toy bear is named 'Teddy's Bear' in honour of President Theodore Roosevelt.

1903 In March Richard Steiff receives an American order for 3,000 bears.

1906 First published use of the name 'teddy bear' to describe plush bear mascots and toys in the November and December editions of the American toy trade magazine *Playthings*.

1907 First animated teddy-bear cartoon, *Little Johnny and the Teddy Bears*, made in the United States.

1907 Dean's Rag Book Company in England publishes a rag book entitled *Teddy Bear* by Alice Scott, illustrated by Sybil Scott Paley.

1907 American composer J. K. Bratton writes 'The Teddy Bear Two Step'. This becomes 'The Teddy Bear's Picnic' when words are added in 1930.

1908 J. K. Farnell makes the first British plush, jointed teddy bear.

1908 Dean's Rag Book Company advertises its first 'cut-out-and-sew' rag teddy bears.

1910 'The Bruin Boys' first appear in Arthur Mee's *Children's Encyclopaedia*.

STEIFF – A NAME TO RECKON WITH

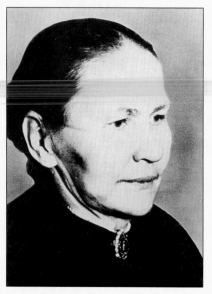

ABOVE: MARGARETE STEIFF. BELOW: A RARE COMPLETE SET OF STEIFF BEAR SKITTLES MADE IN THE 1890S.

No German toy company has done more for the popularity of the teddy bear than Steiff. Those who dispute Morris Michtom's claim to have produced the first genuine teddy bear point to the longer history of the Steiff company, and the bear toys they produced at the end of the nineteenth century.

Margarete Steiff was born in 1847 in Giengen, which is where the company is still based. As a very young child she contracted polio but, despite being wheelchair-bound, she earned her living as a seamstress. At first she worked in people's homes, but soon branched out into selling felt clothing by mail order. From the left-over felt she made elephant-shaped pin cushions from a commercial pattern. These sold so well that toys gradually replaced clothes as the main source of income. In 1893 the company name was changed from The Felt Mail Order Company to The Felt Toy Company.

The range of animals, and of the fabrics used to make them, was widened. Bears at this stage were only a small part of the output. The first Steiff catalogue in 1892 shows clearly that Steiff's early bear toys, although soft filled and made of mohair plush or fur, were not 'teddy' bears but representations of wild bears. They did not have movable, jointed limbs but stood rigid on all fours or on their hind legs. Pull-along bears on metal wheels, revolving bears on metal discs, ride-on bears, chained dancing bears and roly-poly bears on conical wooden bases were all available well before 1902. Among the most famous early Steiff bears are the sets of bear skittles.

The turning point for the Steiff bear came at the end of 1902, at about the same time Teddy Roosevelt's name was being given to the new toy made by Rose Michtom. Richard Steiff, Margarete Steiff's nephew, had designed a new, stuffed plush bear with the added novelty of movable joints. No examples of this original German teddy bear remain. The only record is a photograph in the 1903–4 Steiff catalogue and the catalogue code number 55PB.

The fortunes of the Steiff company were changed by 55PB. Initially the bear was a failure in the company's showroom in New York where it was sent at the end of 1902. It was rejected as being too expensive as well as being too large, too heavy and too unappealing to children. This is why doubts remain about its claim to be the very first teddy bear. Teddy bears should, of course, be very appealing indeed.

The samples were shipped back to Germany and taken to the Leipzig Toy Fair in March 1903. There again they did not create much interest. As the fair drew to a close and the Steiff toys were being packed away, Hermann Berg, a buyer from the George Bergfeldt department store in New York, came along looking for a novelty toy for the next Christmas season. Richard Steiff showed him the bear and Berg ordered

3,000 on the spot! As a result Steiff broke into the American teddy-bear market and found themselves perfectly positioned to exploit the teddy-bear craze.

At this stage the Steiff bear was not yet the perfect teddy bear we know today. Richard Steiff, ever the perfectionist, realised that bear 55PB still had some way to go. So he went and observed bear cubs at Stuttgart Zoo and gradually evolved a younger looking, more doll-like version of his first bear. The stuffing was a softer mixture of wood-wool and kapok. Visually it had something of the sweetness of the American bears but it retained the distinctive realism that distinguishes Steiff bears of the pre-1914 period. In the Steiff catalogues the new softer bear-doll was called Bärle.

One of Richard Steiff's main challenges was to find a safe yet economical way of giving the bears movable joints. The limbs of the very first bears had been attached to the body quite simply, using string or, later, wire. Using this method the limbs easily worked loose. An experimental attempt using metal rods was also tried. The solution Richard Steiff came up with in 1905 was disc jointing. Heavy cardboard discs were placed inside the four corners of the body and in each of the bear's limbs. The limbs were then attached firmly to the body by a pin passing through both discs. This is the method still used today.

Variations based on Bärle, but with the new disc jointing, formed the basis of Steiff's commercial success up until 1914. These variations included mechanical bears, dressed bears and bears in unusual colours of mohair plush. Although the bear's design remained fairly consistent, the name Bärle was quickly dropped and replaced by the universally recognised 'teddy bear'. The years 1903–8 became known as the *Bärenjahre* in the company's history. In 1907 alone, Steiff sold 974,000 bears in the United States and transformed the fortunes of the small German town where they were based.

A problem of Steiff's success was the number of firms which sought to exploit it by making similar bears. Steiff attempted, but failed, to patent the name 'Teddy Bear'. They even tried to patent a growler which would say the word 'Teddy'. Forced to accept that others could, and would, make similar toys, Steiff decided to find a method of identifying their own products while at the same time making sure that the quality was so superior that people would positively seek them out.

Another of Margarete Steiff's nephews, Franz, came up with a solution — an identifying button in the left ear of every Steiff toy. The button and the phrase 'Button in Ear' (*Knopf im Ohr*) were patented at the end of 1904. When rival firms later tried to use a similar system of identification they found that Steiff always challenged any wording using the word 'button', any identifying feature fixed to the ear, and the use of a button placed on any part of the body.

Steiff ear buttons are useful in dating bears. At various times they have been stamped with the original Steiff Elephant Logo (1904–5), been left blank (1905–9, 1948–50 – blue colour, and on seconds since 1984) or stamped with the name Steiff in a variety of scripts.

A WHITE STEIFF TEDDY BEAR C.1908, DRESSED IN A SAILOR SUIT.

A BLUE PLUSH STEIFF TEDDY BEAR MADE IN THE 1920S.

The Golden Age of the Teddy Bear

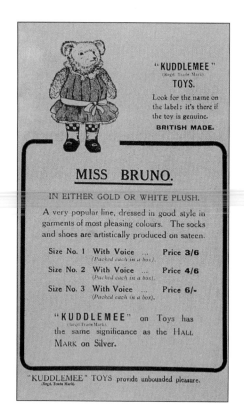

"KUDDLEMEE"
(Regd. Trade Mark)
TOYS.
Look for the name on
the label; it's there if
the toy is genuine.
BRITISH MADE.

MISS BRUNO.

IN EITHER GOLD OR WHITE PLUSH.

A very popular line, dressed in good style in
garments of most pleasing colours. The socks
and shoes are artistically produced on sateen.

Size No. 1 With Voice ... Price 3/6
        (Packed each in a box).
Size No. 2 With Voice ... Price 4/6
        (Packed each in a box).
Size No. 3 With Voice ... Price 6/-
        (Packed each in a box).

"KUDDLEMEE" on Toys has
(Regd. Trade Mark)
the same significance as the HALL
MARK on Silver.

"KUDDLEMEE" TOYS provide unbounded pleasure.
(Regd. Trade Mark)

ABOVE: A PAGE FROM THE 1915
DEAN'S CATALOGUE.
RIGHT: THE PRODUCTION LINE
AT THE DEAN'S FACTORY AT
MERTON, NEAR WIMBLEDON.
THE COMPANY WAS BASED
THERE FROM 1935 TO 1955.

*Here is Edward Bear, coming
downstairs now, bump, bump, on the
back of his head, behind Christopher
Robin . . . here he is at the bottom,
and ready to be introduced to you.
Winnie-the-Pooh.*

A. A. Milne, *Winnie-the-Pooh*, 1926

OPPOSITE: A MUCH-LOVED,
MUCH-MENDED 1920S FARNELL
BEAR.

THE YEAR 1914 saw the outbreak of the First World War, which ravaged Europe for four years, with economic consequences that were still felt many years later. The toy industry did not go untouched. Steiff, and other German manufacturers, had their factories turned over to war work. Exports were inevitably halted. As a result, countries which had relied on imported German teddy bears began to develop and expand their own local soft-toy industries.

Several of the most famous British manufacturers of the inter-war years made their first jointed, plush teddy bears in response to the ban on German bears.

Harwin and Company was founded in 1914. This company made a speciality of dressed bears, including bears kitted out in military uniforms. The first 'Chad Valley' bears were made in 1915 by Johnson Brothers. The Chiltern Toy Works, founded by the teddy bear importer Josef Eisenmann in 1908, also produced their first bear in 1915. He was a dressed bear called Master Teddy, who came in five sizes. To economise on expensive mohair plush the clothed parts of his body were made of cotton.

Dean's advertised their first plush bears in their 1915 'Kuddlemee' catalogue. At this stage bears were only a minor item in the catalogue and regrettably no examples of these pioneer bears, 'Master Bruno' and 'Miss Bruno', have been positively identified.

After the hiatus of 1914–18, the 1920s and 1930s proved to be a Golden Age for the teddy bear worldwide, both in terms of good design and also of financial success.

TRADE MARK.

A1 TEDDY BEARS.
FULLY JOINTED, SOFT AND CUDDLEY.

All sizes in the 1st Grade range are STUFFED BEST KAPOK, the softest, lightest and most hygienic filling material known.

A1 TEDDY BEARS.
FULLY JOINTED, SOFT AND CUDDLEY.

The 2nd Grade range, except No. 9c, is stuffed Wood-wool, which is surpassed as a filler only by the more expensive Kapok.

1st Grade

KAPOK STUFFED.

SOFT LIGHT HYGIENIC.

Size No.	Height about.	Colours.	Plush.	Fitted with.	Boxed for the Trade.	Cable Code.
11 A	11½"	*Gold, Rose Pink or Saxe Blue	1st Grade	Squeak	⅓ dozen	PABAT
12 A	12½"	,,	,,	,,	¼ ,,	PABBY
13 A	13½"	,,	,,	,,	¼ ,,	PABCA
14 A	14½"	,,	,,	,,	¼ ,,	PABDO
16 A	16"	,,	,,	Growler	Singly	PABEL
19 A	19"	,,	,,	,,	,,	PABGU
22 A	22"	,,	,,	,,	,,	PABHE
25 A	25"	,,	,,	,,	,,	PABID
		*State colours required. Assorted colours sent unless otherwise ordered.				
9 C	9"	Gold only	2nd Grade	Squeak	1 dozen	PACCE
10 C	10"	,,	,,	,,	½ ,,	PACDO
11 C	11½"	,,	,,	,,	⅓ ,,	PACET
12 C	12½"	,,	,,	,,	⅓ ,,	PACFY
14 C	14"	,,	,,	,,	¼ ,,	PABKI
16 C	16"	,,	,,	,,	Singly	PABMS

HYGIENIC STUFFING

DEAN'S RAG BOOK Co. Ltd., Elephant & Castle, London, S.E.1.

It was during this period that the French teddy-bear industry evolved. Dozens of small factories flourished, some more notable than others. Marcel Pintel had begun making mechanical bear toys around 1913. In 1919 he produced his first mohair plush bears. Also in 1919, as the country emerged from the devastation of war, Emile Thiennot set up a teddy-bear factory in the Champagne region of France. FADAP (Fabrication Artistique d'Animaux en Peluche) began making bears in 1925. ALFA (Article de Luxe Fabrication Artisanale) produced their first bears in 1936. Unusually for French bears, ALFA bears had open mouths with large smiles. Otherwise one of the typical features of French bears of this period is the sad downturn to their mouths. Other typical features are joint discs which show on the outside of the bear and ears lined with fabric of a contrasting colour.

In the 1920s Australian firms were set up to make bears from imported British mohair. These early Australian bears have become very collectable. Joy Toys, based in Melbourne, was probably the first. Their bears were handmade and traditional in style (although in the 1930s they ceased to have jointed necks). Other collectable bears from Australian firms from between the wars include Emil Toys and the Fideston Toy Company.

In 1919, as the restrictions and raw material shortages caused by the war eased, the newly established British teddy-bear companies were poised for success. They expanded rapidly and created distinctive

ABOVE: A 1930S BLUE PLUSH BEAR MADE BY DEAN'S.

BELOW: TWO BRITISH BEARS MADE IN THE 1930S – LEFT, BY MERRYTHOUGHT, RIGHT BY CHAD VALLEY.

new ranges. J. K. Farnell introduced their Alpha bears around 1920 and registered the Alpha trademark in 1925. In August 1921, A. A. Milne's wife, Daphne, bought an Alpha bear for the first birthday of their son Christopher, and set in train the events that led to the creation of the legendary Winnie-the-Pooh. Farnell bears were renowned for their sparkling eyes and beautiful, silky, long mohair. Even today, after over seventy years of playing and cuddling, Farnell bears retain a luminous quality which makes them stand out.

Dean's also introduced a new range, their A1 bears. However, dolls still remained Dean's main speciality so their teddy bears from this period are quite hard to track down and identify.

Leon Rees, who inherited the Chiltern Toy Works from his father-in-law, Josef Eisenmann, joined forces with Harry Stone of J. K. Farnell to form H. G. Stone and Company. They decided to exploit Eisenmann's original trademark and began marketing themselves as Chiltern Toys in 1923, registering the name in 1924. In 1923 they too introduced a new range, their Hugmee bears, which enjoyed enormous success. Hugmee bears were made in a wide variety of styles, colours and fabrics over the next forty years, and their excellent quality makes them very popular with collectors.

THE TEDDY BEAR HALL OF FAME

The inter-war years were also a truly golden period for Chad Valley. Founded as Johnson Brothers, in 1920 they adopted their trademark as the official company name, becoming the Chad Valley Company, Ltd. In the same year they moved to Shropshire to take over the Wrekin Toy works. In 1931 they also took over Peacock and Company, and began producing the lovely, distinctive Peacock bears, with their traditional big chunky bodies, broad faces with pointed, shaved snouts and large cupped ears. Chad Valley bears were chosen to advertise Bear Brand Stockings, which proved good publicity for both firms. Even better publicity was the fact that Chad Valley bears were favourites of the Duchess of York, later Queen

Elizabeth, who bought them for her daughters, the Princesses Elizabeth and Margaret. Chad Valley were granted the Royal Warrant in 1938 and added 'Toymakers to Her Majesty the Queen' to their labels from that year.

New British companies dating from this period include Pixie Toys, Invicta Toys and Pedigree Soft Toys, which was established in 1937 by the large toy and nursery furniture company, Lines Brothers. But the new firm which has best stood the test of time is Merrythought, which was set up in Shropshire in 1930. With the expertise of a production director from Chad Valley (C. J. Rendle) and a sales director from J. K. Farnell (A. C. Janisch), it is not surprising that by 1935 they were claiming to be the largest soft-toy factory in the country. All early

TWO VERSIONS OF STEIFF'S SUCCESSFUL DESIGN, TEDDY BABY, WHICH FIRST APPEARED IN 1929.

Merrythought bears are attractive and collectable. They include the Bingie bear cubs produced between 1931 and 1938 and the plump bears with fat thighs, broad faces and large flat ears, initially known as Magnet bears, which were clearly influenced by neighbouring Chad Valley.

In the United States, which was relatively untouched by the First World War, the teddy-bear industry had continued to prosper. Names of American manufacturers of this period include the Knickerbocker Toy Company, which began making bears around 1920, and Gund which, although it was founded in about 1906, only began manufacturing in any real quantity in the 1930s. However the devastating effect of the Great Depression, which began with the Wall Street Crash in 1929, forced many manufacturers into making cheaper bears. These distinctive American mass-market bears were cut with straight bodies and limbs, to use fabric as economically as possible, and they were noticeably thin. As a result they are known to collectors today as 'Stick Bears'.

After a few difficult years the German toy industry was back on its feet by the early 1920s. Steiff, which between 1919 and 1921 had been reduced to making its bears from inferior, prickly, paper plush, began to produce high-quality mohair bears again from the beginning of 1920. As always they worked hard to stay one jump ahead of the competition with a series of innovative designs, although the departure of Richard Steiff to oversee the American side of the business deprived them of their foremost designer. He sent back a strong message that the American market required a softer, jollier, smiling product decorated with ribbons and in brighter, less realistic colours. Steiff design innovations of this period all aimed to create colourful, softer, more doll-like bears. These include Teddy Clown (1926), the bear baby 'Petsy' (1928) and 'Teddy Baby' – 'a comical young bear cub' (1929).

The Hermann family also enjoyed great success in the inter-war years. The sons and daughter of toymaker Johann Hermann all went into the toy trade. Adelheid, Artur and Max made the

*Every child should be able to
distinguish our products from those of
our competitors, even at a distance.*

Richard Steiff, 1925

family's first teddy bear in 1913, while running a small company from their father's
house. Artur later founded the firm Artur Hermann. After the First World War,
another brother, Bernhard Hermann, founded the firm which, under the direction
of his sons, became known as Gebrüder Hermann in 1951. To this day it has
remained a family firm run by Bernhard Hermann's grand-daughters. Max set up
a company in 1920 which eventually became Hermann Spielwaren. It too continues to trade as a family firm. All the Hermann companies enjoyed success in the
Golden Age of the teddy bear and developed distinctive styles. They became the
main rivals to Steiff and it is often hard to tell their bears apart unless the labels
remain. One area of difference is that Hermann teddies tend to have snouts made
of a different fabric and colour from the rest of the body. They are frequently
designed with the mouth open, a feature not often found outside Germany.

Another successful German company during the 1920s and 1930s was
Schreyer and Company which adopted the Schuco trademark in 1921. The
company made attractive conventional bears in long mohair but also made a
speciality of mechanical and novelty bears. In 1921 they introduced their famous

Yes/No bear, an amusing combination of the traditional and the mechanical. Its head could nod or shake from side to side using a mechanism operated by a lever in the tail. This device was used in many styles of Schuco bear and the British company, Chiltern Toys, introduced a version in 1937 which they called the Wagmee bear.

Schuco were also renowned for their miniature bears, structured around wire frames and made from clipped-down mohair to keep the fur in scale with the bears. There were many novelty miniatures, including tumbling mechanical miniatures, miniatures in unusual colours such as lilac and lime-green, and miniatures which hid surprises like perfume phials, a lipstick and powder compact or even a tiny pot of jam. All are greatly valued by collectors and fetch consistently high prices.

Design features of this period in bears of all origins are the use of glass eyes, the introduction in the mid 1920s of dual-coloured mohair, the fashion for bears made from art-silk plush (artificial silk made from cotton or wood pulp), the continual move away from realism – humps became something of a rarity – and the introduction of new softer fillings with tradenames like Chad Valley's Aerolite.

The Far East was less heavily involved in soft-toy manufacturing between the wars than might have been expected. Although some bears were produced in Japan, these were generally of poor quality and they made little impact. People still preferred to buy quality hand-finished teddy bears and did so in great numbers. Mass production had not yet wrought its devastating effect on the traditional teddy-bear companies. For them the 1920s and 1930s were indeed their Golden Age.

A TEDDY BEAR HISTORY

SOME TEDDY BEAR MILESTONES

1919 Alcock and Brown take teddy-bear mascots made by the British firm Harwin and Co., on the first non-stop flight across the Atlantic.

1919 Britain's first ever comic-strip teddy bear, Bobby Bear, appears in the *Daily Herald*.

1920 Mary Tourtel creates the first Rupert Bear stories for the *Daily Express*.

1924 Walt Disney produces the colour animation film *Alice and the Three Bears*.

1926 A. A. Milne's children's book *Winnie-the-Pooh* is published.

1930 Merrythought soft-toy company goes into production.

1937 Arrival of a giant panda at Chicago Zoo leads to a fashion for panda bears.

Teddy Under Threat

JUST AS IT had done some thirty years previously, in 1945 the teddy-bear industry had to plan recovery after the effects of a world war. The 1940s and 1950s saw many new developments and adaptations to changing circumstances and consumer demands. At first the industry seemed to recover quite well. Chiltern Toys actually expanded immediately following the end of the war. Eventually, however, it became clear that a new economic threat was an even greater cause for concern than the legacy of the war.

One of the main post-war developments was the increased use of synthetic fibres and stuffing. These included acrylic plush and nylon plush. Acrylic and nylon fibres had both been invented before the war and their use had been developed and accelerated during the war years. Afterwards they became important in the commercial market. Foam rubber became a standard choice for stuffing soft toys. It was produced under a number of different tradenames but all were variations on the same basic product. In its granulated form it was particularly suitable for making washable toys.

Demand for hygienic, washable toys was a big impetus for the use of artificial fibres. In 1954 Wendy Boston, an English firm, patented a fully washable teddy. The firm had already patented lock-in safety eyes. Washability and synthetics affected the styling and appearance of the bears. But the threat of competition from the soft-toy industry in the Far East had an even greater influence on style.

In the 1950s and 1960s the Far East's phenomenal success in exporting cheap, synthetic, mass-produced toys hit at the heart of the traditional soft-toy industry with its emphasis on quality and expensive hand-finishing. Even the most well-established firms were not safe. Despite introducing ranges that looked more like the imported soft toys, they were unable to compete on price when labour costs were so much lower in the Far East.

Australian firms were particularly badly hit. Joy Toys stopped production in 1971, although the name was bought by another firm. Many new Australian firms had started up during or just after the war and initially looked set fair for success. These firms included the Verna Toy Company (1941), Lindee Toys (1944) and Barton Waugh (early 1950s). However, because they had initially been protected by import restrictions, they were inadequately prepared for the effects of foreign competition. When restrictions were lifted during the 1960s, and cheap imports flooded in, most traditional firms went out of business. An exception was Jakas Soft Toys (1954) which still exists today and specialises in koala bears.

It was the same sad story elsewhere. In France,

A lovable, but naughty little boy teddy bear of five years old, who gets away with the sorts of things all children would like to. As with Peter Pan, he never gets any older.

Harry Corbett on Sooty

THIS DEAN'S BEAR IS TYPICAL OF THE ARTIFICIAL PLUSH BEARS MADE AFTER THE SECOND WORLD WAR.

Pintel Frères went out of production in the 1960s. FADAP closed down in 1978. ALFA ceased trading sometime in the 1970s. In Germany, Schuco stopped making bears in 1976 when it was sold to Dunbee-Combex-Marx, who sold on the trademark. The once successful Knickerbocker Toy Company in the United States eventually ceased trading completely in the early 1980s.

British firms, which fell victim to the glut of cheap, mass-produced toys, include the Britannia Toy Company, the British United Manufacturing Company (Omega), J. K. Farnell and Company, Ealontoys, Chad Valley (whose tradename was eventually sold for use on toys made in the Far East), Chiltern Toys (taken over initially by Chad Valley), Wendy Boston Playsafe Toys and Pedigree Soft Toys.

The German companies Steiff, Gebrüder Hermann and Hermann Spielwaren were at the forefront of the fight-back, developing styles to compete with the cuddly look of the cheap imports. In 1951, Richard Steiff's classic bear was redesigned with a flatter, rounder face and shorter, straighter limbs. In 1966, this design was made even more cub-like and registered as Original Teddy Bear. In 1951, the Steiff 'Zotty' bear, a super-soft, long-haired bear, was patented. So great was the change in approach that many of the new Steiff bears did not even have movable joints. Gebrüder Hermann introduced a Zotty-type bear of their own, only distinguishable by the fact that it did not have a white bib like its Steiff counterpart.

Although companies like Steiff and Hermann in Germany and Dean's, Lefray and Merrythought in Britain did manage to keep going, in the 1970s prospects looked very bleak indeed. Yet just when things seemed at their worst a change of fortune was in the air. It is a great sadness that so many long-established firms went out of business without being able to reap the benefits of the renewed fervour for traditional, handmade teddy bears which was just around the corner.

Mr and Mrs Brown first met Paddington on a railway platform. In fact, that was how he came to have such an unusual name for a bear, for Paddington was the name of the station.

Michael Bond, *A Bear Called Paddington*, 1958

SOME TEDDY BEAR MILESTONES

1944 Smokey Bear becomes the mascot for the United States Forest Fire Prevention Campaign.

1952 Sooty first appears on British television.

1954 Wendy Boston produces the first completely washable teddy bear made from nylon plush and stuffed with foam rubber.

1958 *A Bear Called Paddington* by Michael Bond is published.

1960 Walt Disney Company acquires the rights to Winnie-the-Pooh and makes the first full-length Winnie-the-Pooh film in 1975.

THE TEDDY BEAR HALL OF FAME

The Teddy Bear Revival

T HE END OF the 1960s and the early 1970s were dark days for the traditional, handmade teddy bear. But a bright future was just around the corner.

Those, like the poet John Betjeman, who retained a devotion to their teddy bears well into adulthood, began to show their true colours. Men and women who had owned teddy bears in the pioneering years at the beginning of the century found the cuddly charms of mass-produced soft toys no substitute for the robust individuality of the real thing. A demand for genuine, traditional teddy bears began to make itself felt. It was a demand that came from adults rather than children. Real teddy bears were coming back into fashion, not simply as children's toys, but as desirable collectables for grown-ups.

There are several people who played an important role in re-awakening the dormant love for old and traditional bears.

'When, as a boy, I came home from school and found that my mother had given my Teddy Bear away to a jumble sale, I had a distinct sense of bereavement.' So wrote Peter Bull, the man who probably did most to arrest the decline of the traditional teddy bear. After making this confession in front of millions on American television he received over 2,000 letters of support. This prompted him to write a book on the subject. In order to do so he advertised widely for teddy-bear stories and memorabilia and was astounded at the response. The book, entitled *Bear With Me* (later called *The Teddy Bear Book*) came out in 1969 and was an immediate success.

Peter Bull's openness about his love for teddy bears inspired others. One of the most influential was the American Jim Ownby. After reading Peter Bull's book he founded a charitable organisation called Good Bears of the World to unite bear lovers internationally and to give sick children and adults the comfort of a teddy bear. This put him in touch with Colonel Bob Henderson, a teddy-bear collector who already ran an informal teddy-bear club himself from his Edinburgh home. Colonel Henderson took over the running of the British branch of Good Bears of the World.

Extra impetus was given to the interest in old bears by the worldwide success of the television serialisation of Evelyn Waugh's novel, *Brideshead Revisited*, in 1981. One of the main characters, Sebastian Flyte, has a great attachment to his childhood bear. The bear chosen for the television role was an early American bear belonging to Peter Bull, called Delicatessen, and he became a star in his own right.

By the early 1980s old teddies had become hot news and a recognised form of collectable. Teddy-bear collectors had acquired a new name – arctophiles (from the Greek words *arctos*, meaning bear and *philos*, meaning lover), and teddy-bear collecting had become arctophilia. The trend got under way first in the United States, which was at least six or seven years ahead of the rest of the world.

Teddy Bears are so much cheaper than a psychiatrist, and not nearly so supercilious.

Peter Bull

My teddy bear was the very first masculine love of my life.

Barbara Cartland

What do you suppose Lord Sebastian wanted? A hair brush for his Teddy-bear; it had to have very stiff bristles, not, Lord Sebastian said, to brush him with, but to threaten him with a spanking when he was sulky.

Evelyn Waugh, *Brideshead Revisited*, 1945

THE THREE STARS OF *Brideshead Revisited*: JEREMY IRONS, ANTHONY ANDREWS AND DELICATESSEN AS ALOYSIUS.

MERRYTHOUGHT'S WELLINGTON
WEARING A MERRYTHOUGHT
TEDDY BEAR PURSE.

Early bears were no longer discarded but revived by their loving owners or sold by people who recognised their new market value. As a result early bears became scarce and their prices went up. It was at this stage that the traditional toy makers were able to step into the breach and provide alternatives and new types of bear to meet the ever-increasing demands of the collectors' market.

The collectors' market for *new* bears is based on the creation of Limited Editions which are eagerly snapped up and which eventually acquire a resale value of their own. Some of these are entirely new designs. Others, called Replica Bears, are based on patterns of bears made by the company many years earlier. Steiff has made a feature of Limited Editions and of Limited Edition Replica Bears. Among its most successful Limited Editions have been the copy of the 1928 Teddy Clown, re-created in an edition of 11,020, replicas of the 1930 Teddy Baby (7,000 each of the boy and the girl) and a 1985 replica of the 1930 Dicky Bear in a world edition of 20,000.

The old-established firms have underlined their history by producing special bears to celebrate their anniversaries. For example, in 1990 Hermann made a 75th Anniversary bear and Merrythought made a 60th Anniversary bear. Sometimes anniversary bears are new designs, sometimes they are replicas from the original year. Both Steiff and Gebrüder Hermann produced beautiful bears to celebrate the reunification of Germany.

It is very important that collectors who are investing in these new bears, rather than buying them as toys, should preserve their value by keeping them, and their boxes, in perfect condition and making sure that all identifying labels and tags remain intact and with the bear.

ABOVE: A TEDDY BEAR
PASSPORT FOR THE BEAR THAT
LIKES TO TRAVEL.
RIGHT: A CAROUSEL OF
MERRYTHOUGHT 'CHEEKIES'
(1995).

THE TEDDY BEAR HALL OF FAME

Seeing the success of the established firms, new companies began to set themselves up to create the same sort of traditional bears. Each new company intended to give their bears a unique appeal, which made them essential for all serious collectors. The North American Bear Company in the United States, and Nonsuch and Canterbury bears in England are good examples of creative new teddy-bear firms.

I heard the church bells hollowing out the sky,
Deep beyond deep, like never-ending stars,
And turned to Archibald, my safe old bear,
Whose woollen eyes looked sad or glad at me,
Whose half-moon ears received my confidence,
Who made me laugh, who never let me down.
I used to wait for hours to see him move,
Convinced that he could breathe.

John Betjeman (1906–84) on his beloved bear Archibald, recalled in *Summoned by Bells*, 1960

RIGHT: A HERMANN UNIFICATION BEAR GIVEN TO THE MUSEUM IN 1995 BY EAST BERLINERS JOCHEN AND JUTTA FRANK. THE FRANKS WERE IN TOUCH WITH THE MUSEUM BEFORE THE WALL CAME DOWN. IN 1989 THEY HANDED OVER A BEAR AT CHECKPOINT CHARLIE AS A GESTURE OF EAST-WEST FRIENDSHIP.

SOME TEDDY BEAR MILESTONES

1964 *The Book of The Teddy Bear* by Margaret Hutchings is published.

1969 Publication of *Bear With Me* (*The Teddy Bear Book*, USA) by Peter Bull.

1973 American Jim Ownby launches Good Bears of the World.

1979 'Great Teddy Bear Rally' held at Longleat House, home of the Marquess of Bath. More than 18,000 people and their bears attend.

1981 Peter Bull's bear, Delicatessen, stars as Aloysius in the BBC TV adaptation of Evelyn Waugh's *Brideshead Revisited*.

1981 The term 'Bear Artist' is first used in the United States in the magazine *Doll Reader*.

1983 Sotheby's include teddy bears in their collectors' auctions for the first time.

Teddy Bear Artists

The Teddy Bear is the King of stuffed beasts and all other toys.

National Geographic Magazine, November, 1974

OPPOSITE: THE TEDDY BEAR WEDDING IN THE MUSIC ROOM AT THE MUSEUM — ALL THESE BEARS ARE THE WORK OF LEADING CONTEMPORARY BRITISH BEAR MAKERS.

BELOW: A MODERN BRITISH BEAR BY BEAR-ARTIST SUE QUINN OF DORMOUSE DESIGNS.

A NEW PHENOMENON, which also began in the United States, was the emergence of bear artists. These are people who make individual bears by hand. Sometimes they make just one unique bear, sometimes a small number of the same design. This is an entirely new aspect of teddy-bear collecting. The joy of bear artists is that they can produce bears with very different styles and personalities without having to produce in the sort of numbers required to keep a company with many employees afloat.

Most bear artists actually work at home and sell their bears direct to customers at teddy-bear festivals and

OPPOSITE: THE VICTORIAN
DOLL'S HOUSE IN THE MUSEUM
LIBRARY FEATURES A
COLLECTION OF MINIATURE
BEARS. SEEN HERE IS THE
FAMILY OF TINY WELSH BEARS
MADE BY BEAR-ARTIST SUE
SCHOEN.

fairs. Collectors cherish these bears because of their individuality, and there is already a market to sell them on at auction. It would be impossible to list all the people now making handcrafted bears. In the twenty-five years or so since the first bear artists began operating in the United States a number of names have become particularly prominent. These include Pam Howells (who used to design for Chiltern Toys), Jo Greeno, June Kendall and Gregory Gyllenship in England; Su Lain, Dee Hockenberry and Ted Menten in the United States.

Recently larger companies have commissioned designs from bear artists to manufacture in larger quantities. For instance, Naomi Laight and Janet Clark have designed bears for Dean's to make in Limited Editions of 1,500.

A whole new industry has grown up around the traditional teddy bear, with magazines, books, conventions, fairs, festivals, picnics, shops, museums, CD-ROMs, new manufacturers, bear artists and auctions. It seems that as the teddy bear approaches its century it remains more youthful and full of life than ever.

When you're feeling lonely, when you're feeling down,
When your little face is furrowed with a frown,
When you're feeling fed-up, when you're feeling grey,
When you're feeling tongue-tied and don't know what to say,
What's the answer? It's a bear!

Gyles Brandreth, 'What's the answer? It's a bear!', 1995

THE
TEDDY
BEAR
GALLERY

The Principal Bears

Teddy Girl

TEDDY GIRL is a beautiful brown Steiff bear made in about 1904. She belonged to the late Colonel Bob Henderson, a distinguished army officer who had served throughout the First World War with the support of a small teddy-bear mascot in his rucksack. Despite his tough army background Colonel Bob was a pioneer of what he called 'Teddy Bear Consciousness' – the power of this unique cuddly toy to unlock reserves of goodwill and kindness in all sorts of very different people.

In 1962, seven years after retiring from the army, Colonel Bob started the Teddy Bear Club. He later set up and ran the British branch of Good Bears of the World, the charity founded by American Jim Ownby. As a result he became an international focus for fellow teddy-bear enthusiasts.

During the colonel's childhood his bear was known as Teddy Boy. However, Colonel Bob's daughter, who loved the bear as much as her father had done, brought about a change of gender by dressing the bear in a frock and renaming her Teddy Girl.

In December 1994, following the colonel's death, his famous collection of over 600 bears was sold. Teddy Girl entered the record books by fetching the highest price ever for a teddy bear sold at auction, a staggering £110,000. Her new owner is Japanese toy-factory owner Yoshihiro Sekiguchi.

Teddy Girl now takes pride of place in Mr Sekiguchi's Teddy Bear Museum in Izu, Japan.

Metal Rod Bear

THIS LITTLE BEAR is one of The Teddy Bear Museum's most important residents. He is no ordinary bear but a rare, metal-rodded bear with the Steiff code 28PB.

Movable arms and legs were essential for a true teddy bear, but finding a method that was practical, safe and not over-expensive was a major challenge. Richard Steiff, Margarete Steiff's invaluable nephew, experimented with several methods of creating movable joints which were hard-wearing without being too heavy. The thread used to join body and limbs in Steiff's early bears was easily damaged by an over-enthusiastic young owner. The same method, but using wire, was potentially dangerous, despite the addition of metal caps to cover the ends of the wire. The problem appeared to be solved when on 8 June 1905 Steiff registered the patent for a system of metal rods which were joined, like axles, through the arms, legs and neck joint. This worked extremely well, but it made the bears rather heavy and was very expensive. As a result the metal-rod bears were only made during the year 1905. Their rarity makes them much sought after by today's collectors.

Of additional interest is the fact that our small bear retains his original boot-button eyes and the distinctive nose of sealing wax (gutta-percha) which was a distinguishing feature of all the metal-rodded bears. Bears like this were given the new Steiff trademark button, marked with an embossed elephant, which had been registered in December 1904.

Petz

Richard Steiff did not only experiment with the technical aspects of the teddy bears' construction. He was also constantly re-assessing their appearance and attempting to give them a more doll-like appeal. This bear was made in about 1905, probably as something of an experiment in the never-ending quest to achieve a perfect teddy bear. Although such bears crop up from time to time in sale rooms, their unusual ears, sitting low on the side of the head, distinguish them from the more classic Steiff bears.

The fur is an attractive white-blonde. Blonde plush was extremely popular at this time so the wide-eared bear would have been the height of fashion. His long, thin feet, typical of early Steiff bears, are slightly worn. The underlying red felt shows through, a reminder that Margarete Steiff's business was originally based on making felt clothes and stuffed felt animals. This was a much softer bear than his predecessors.

The bear's construction is revealed by the letters PAB in his code which stand for *Plusch Angeschiebt Beweglich* (plush, disc-jointed, movable). It indicates that the bear has the new disc joints.

The wide-eared bear, like all his disc-jointed contemporaries, with their sweeter faces, was called Bärle. There is also evidence that the familiar children's name for these early German bears was 'Petz'. One thing is certain, in 1905 the name 'teddy bear' had not yet crossed the Atlantic and become universal.

Right from the start the teddy bear was used as a decoration on all sorts of novelty items. Teddy-bear tea services, like this early Steiff set used by bears at the Museum, has become something of a classic in its own right. Steiff still make similar tea services today.

Bärle

ERE WE HAVE a wonderful example of the classic teddy design that Richard Steiff finally settled on and that was initially known, like the earlier models, as Bärle. It was not until 1908 that Steiff conceded to the trans-Atlantic name and called its bear Teddy-Bär.

All the requisite classic Steiff features are clearly here: a protruding, shaved muzzle with stitched snout, a hump back, long arms with spoon-shaped paws, narrow ankles with long thin feet, straw stuffing and swivel disc joints. His eyes are wooden boot buttons, painted black, and attached to the head by metal loops on the back. Almost all early Steiff bears have these boot-button eyes, although a few bears with glass eyes were made before 1920, mainly for the British market.

Our furry friend is a cinnamon long-plush teddy, dating probably from 1905. Cinnamon plush is unusual and very desirable in a bear of this age. He also has the extra rarity value of being a 'centre-seam' bear. These bears were the seventh made from a standard roll of plush. In order to avoid any waste of the expensive material, the seventh bear was squeezed out of the roll by giving it a face made from two pieces, not one. This meant it had a seam down the centre of the muzzle, a non-standard feature which adds to its value.

The Steiff button can be seen clearly in the left ear of our Bärle. A small number of the very first buttons used in 1904 were blank, but almost immediately they were followed by buttons with the original Steiff trademark – an elephant with an S-shaped trunk. The embossed word

Steiff, with the elongated final F, which is shown here, was first used in 1905. Variations on this button design were used until 1950. Retaining the original button after ninety years is a real bonus and gives extra value to any bear. However, even without his ear button, this handsome character would be a very desirable addition to any collection.

Baby Bärle

ANOTHER VERSION of the classic bear, which was made by Steiff right up to 1951, is this enchanting small (33 cm/13 in) Bärle. It was introduced as a novelty by Richard Steiff, in 1905, and boasted the extra attraction of a growler. Paul Steiff, one of Richard's brothers, had introduced the concept of growlers which worked by being tipped forwards and backwards, in addition to the original squeeze-box or drawstring systems. Sadly, as is usually the case with very old bears, the growler in this bear no longer operates. Baby Bärle's nose has the horizontal stitching used by Steiff on their smaller bears: larger bears have vertical nose stitching.

This bear, which lives in the Museum, was probably made in 1906. We know that bears of this size were very popular in England and in 1908 Margarete Steiff was asked to send over a special order of them. Otto Steiff, another of Margarete Steiff's hard-working nephews, was in London in 1908 to drum up extra business because the United States, Steiff's main outlet, was suffering from a temporary economic recession. One of the marketing methods Otto Steiff used was postcards printed with teddy-bear scenes. These postcards have now become collectables in their own right.

Aloysius

Aloysius is one of the bears who helped change teddy-bear history. An early American Ideal bear, he began life in 1907. After his owner grew up he sat on a shelf in a grocery store in Sacco, Maine, for over fifty years. In 1969 this owner, Euphemia Ladd, saw Peter Bull with his bears on an American television programme, and sent her bear to him as a very welcome present. Because of the bear's origins, Peter Bull gave him the name Delicatessen.

When the television serial of Evelyn Waugh's *Brideshead Revisited* was planned Peter Bull was contacted and asked if he could lend a bear to play the part of Aloysius, the childhood bear of the young aristocrat Sebastian Flyte. Peter Bull offered Delicatessen, who gave a successful audition and got the part. The television programmes in 1981 were an amazing success in both Britain and the United States and Delicatessen became, almost overnight, a star bear.

As a result of his success in the role of Aloysius it was decided to accept that bear and acting role had become synonymous in the minds of the public and Delicatessen's name was officially changed, by deed poll, to Aloysius.

For some years after Peter Bull's death Aloysius lived at The Teddy Bear Museum. Following a spell with American bear collectors, Rosemary and Paul Volpp, he can now be found at Teddy Bears of Witney.

IN 1984 the North American Bear Company produced an unjointed brown bear with a soft stuffing which they called Aloysius in honour of Waugh's literary bear. In 1987, The House of Nisbet made an exact replica of the original 1907 Ideal bear used in the television serial. As we can see here, even the patches and mends on the bear's paws were reproduced exactly as on the original. To create the effect of age a new fabric called distressed mohair was devised by House of Nisbet owner, Jack Wilson. This has since become a standard fabric among bear makers. As a final touch, the bear was given a scarf like the one worn by the original Aloysius for his starring role in *Brideshead Revisited*.

Because the North American Bear Company owned copyright of the name Aloysius, The House of Nisbet reverted to the original name and called their replica Delicatessen.

THE TEDDY BEAR HALL OF FAME

Alfonzo

IN 1908 the Grand Duke George Mikhailovich of Russia commissioned a red mohair Steiff bear for his four-year-old daughter, the Princess Xenia Georgievna. This order was unusual, for although the bear was in the classic Steiff design and a standard size (33 cm/13 in), the most popular colours at this time were dark brown, light brown, blonde and white. The Princess's cousin, the Tsarevitch Alexei Romanov, owned a traditional Steiff bear several sizes larger but in brown plush.

The Princess's nanny dressed her bear in the orange tunic and trousers of one of the Tsar's privileged Cossack horsemen and he was given the name Alfonzo. In 1914, he was taken with the Princess on a visit to her English cousins, King George V and his family. Princess Xenia Georgievna never returned to Russia. During her stay in England the First World War broke out and, in 1919, the Grand Duke was murdered at St Petersburg following the 1917 Bolshevik Revolution. Throughout the Princess's exile, until her death in 1965, Alfonzo remained her closest link with home and her old way of life.

The original Alfonzo was left to Princess Xenia Georgievna's daughter and was eventually sold at auction and bought by Teddy Bears of Witney for £12,100 in 1989. Once again the exceptional history of a teddy bear increased its worth beyond its basic market value.

In 1990, Steiff produced an exact replica of Alfonzo, right down to the wood-wool stuffing and Cossack outfit, in a Limited Edition of 5,000. Replica bears like Alfonzo are now a separate collectors' speciality and, if well cared for and kept with their original boxes, their value increases quite rapidly. Steiff have made a speciality of replicas using their original patterns. Most of their early successes have been recycled in this way, like the 1985 replica of the 1930 Dicky Bear and the 1993 replica of the early Bärle 35 PAB.

Smithsonian Bear

THE EARLY American bear in this photograph lives in the prestigious Smithsonian Institute in Washington. There have been rumours that this is the first bear made by the Ideal Novelty and Toy Company and that it was presented to Theodore Roosevelt to thank him for allowing his name to be given to the new stuffed toy.

In fact this is not the original Teddy's bear – no one knows where that is – but a very fine Ideal and Novelty Toy Company bear made some four years or so after the first American teddy, and given to one of the children in the Roosevelt family. It was generously presented to the Smithsonian in 1964 by Theodore Roosevelt's grandson, as a reminder of the link between the teddy bear and the 26th President of the United States.

The rumour that President Roosevelt owned one of the very first bears was probably spread by Morris and Rose Michtom to publicise their new venture, the Ideal Novelty and Toy Company. Morris Michtom claimed he wrote a letter to President Roosevelt, asking his permission to name the new toy after him, and sending him a bear. It is this bear, which has never been found or identified, which is often wrongly assumed to be the bear in the Smithsonian.

Michtom also said he had received a letter back from the President insisting that he could see no value in the name but saying that he was happy for the Michtoms to make use of it if they wished.

It seems unlikely the Michtoms would not have kept something so potentially valuable as the President's letter, if it really existed, and the whole story is probably a fabrication. Nevertheless the bear which now sits in the Smithsonian is an impressive example of an early American bear and his connections with President Roosevelt are certainly closer than those of any other teddy bear.

Teddy-bear Muff

THIS GERMAN blonde plush teddy-bear muff dates from around 1908. He has a black-stitched snout and black shoe-button eyes. The legs are not movable but the arms swivel independently and the front paws have kid-leather pads. He has other telltale details of the kind you would expect from a genuine teddy bear, including stitched claws on the round feet and neatly stitched, cup-shaped ears.

The date places him right at the beginning of the teddy-bear craze. Even ninety years ago teddy bears were being adapted for a number of uses beyond simple toys. No doubt mothers (and nannies) before the First World War had the same difficulty persuading children to stay dressed warmly as they do today. A teddy-bear muff was a perfect incentive to keep little hands tucked away out of the cold. We can see that this muff was well used by the wear on the plush around its square middle.

Teddy-bear muffs are still made as novelty items today, notably by Steiff and by Merrythought, although muffs are no longer an everyday form of clothing. Ear muffs, in the form of teddy-bear faces, are a modern variation on the same theme, which reappear every few years.

Somersaulting Bear

THE SOMERSAULTING BEAR was one of Steiff's most successful pre-war bears. The bear is basically the classic small Bärle with the addition of a simple clockwork mechanism. Over 20,000 of them were produced between November 1908, when the patent was first registered, and 1916. Another, smaller, run of them was made in the 1930s and in 1990 a replica edition, limited to 5,000, was produced.

Otto Steiff had seen a mechanical French bear while representing the company in London and wrote to the factory suggesting they produce something similar. Hugo Steiff, brother of Richard, Otto, Paul and Franz, developed a method of using the arms of the bear as an integral wind-up key for the bear's clockwork mechanism.

The bear was initially produced in two sizes and in either light or dark brown or white mohair plush. Later a blonde plush version was made with the British market specifically in mind. The bear shown here is blonde plush and dates from about 1912.

The way in which the bear performed its somersaults was very simple. Its hind legs were put in the sitting position, enabling the long arms to touch the ground. The arms were wound up and as they unwound they tipped the bear forward and over on itself.

A variation on this mechanism was used from 1909–11 to make the Purzel Bär, which turned somersaults while hanging, like a gymnast, from a metal bar.

Pull-along Bear

ADLY THIS BEAR has no identifying button but it is almost certainly a
Steiff pull-along dating from around 1910. Animals on wheels formed a
large proportion of Steiff's production from the company's very earliest
years, well before they started making teddy bears. For a number of years an
elephant on wheels was the Steiff trademark.

This bear's eyes are brown glass, which Steiff sometimes used for the English
market prior to 1914. The four-spoked metal wheels are consistent with the type
used on Steiff pull-alongs of this size and period. From 1914 Steiff introduced
wooden wheels and in the 1920s solid metal disc wheels were used.

The pointed stitched snout and general profile show a marked similarity to the
bears on wheels in Steiff photographs. However, there is no really pronounced
hump so possibly it was a copy made by one of the many other German toy
companies which at this time were exploiting the popularity of Steiff's
traditional designs. Whatever the truth about his origins, our little pull-along is a
very welcome addition to the Museum's collection of early bears.

Alexis Tarnoff's Bear

Tʜɪs ᴅᴇʟɪɢʜᴛꜰᴜʟ bear was presented to the Museum, after Alexis Tarnoff's death in 1989, by his friend, Jean Wilson. Alexis Tarnoff, a dancer, whose photograph was donated along with his bear, was born in 1901, before the appearance of the first teddy bear. He apparently acquired his bear when he was five years old which makes it a very old bear indeed, and one which was clearly much loved.

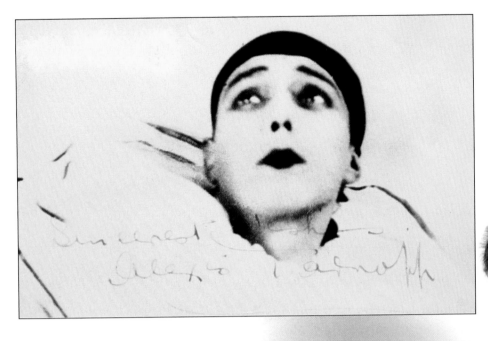

The bear is stuffed with wood-wool, has black, painted boot-button eyes, wool stitched claws on both hands and feet and is made of mohair — all typical features of early bears. However, in some ways he is quite unusual. His narrow arms and legs are attached to his body with exterior metal fastenings, rather like large buttons, which carry the tradename Shield.

In many ways this bear resembles the French teddy bears of the 1920s and 1930s, which often featured similar external jointing. Marcel Pintel's bears had such tapering limbs and firmly stuffed bodies and French bears by other manufacturers were so similar they are impossible to differentiate without their labels. It would have been quite likely that Alexis Tarnoff would own a French bear in addition to his original childhood bear. France was a major dance centre in the 1920s and 1930s and during this period dancers often gave each other small teddy bears as good-luck mascots. Alexis Tarnoff eventually came to live near Manchester where he was well known as a teacher and examiner of ballet.

Perhaps Alexis Tarnoff had two bears and their histories became entangled. Perhaps he was given a bear by a fellow dancer or to replace his lost childhood bear. Perhaps this is quite simply, as stated, his childhood bear. The different possibilities make Alexis Tarnoff's bear particularly fascinating. Trying to solve teddy-bear puzzles like this is one of the reasons collecting teddy bears is such a satisfying hobby.

Black Bear

EVEN QUITE early in their history teddy bears were created in unrealistic colours, such as pink and blue. But usually bears were based on natural colours, in shades of brown, grey, black or white. In the wild, brown bears used to live throughout Europe, and they are still found in Asia and North America. Their close cousins, the Syrian bears, are grey with a white collar. Black bears are natives of North America and the Asiatic black bear is found from Iran and up through the Himalayas, in Burma, Indo-China, Manchuria, Japan and Korea. In the Arctic, white polar bears blend in with the snowy wastes in which they live and hunt.

At various times Steiff have made bears that are based on all these wild bears. One of Richard Steiff's most famous early prototypes was a small grey bear. In 1912, Steiff produced a black mohair bear specifically for the British market. This has become one of the most sought-after additions to any serious collection because the edition was limited to only 494 bears. It was commonly believed at the time that these bears, in their mourning colour, were intended as gifts for those who had lost relatives when the British passenger liner, the *Titanic*, sank in April 1912, while on her maiden voyage.

One of the reasons black teddy bears are less common than the other natural colours is that it is difficult to see the definition of the features in the dark fabric, so the character in their faces can become lost. Steiff attempted to overcome this drawback by setting the eyes in a circle of red felt to make them more prominent. Not all Steiff black bears have the red felt behind their eyes and those that do not have added rarity value and fetch higher prices. Othello, a 1912 Steiff black bear with a centre seam, fetched a record £24,200 for a black bear at Sotheby's in 1990.

Loved to Pieces

THIS THREADBARE bear shows all the signs of having been hugged and cuddled almost to extinction. Like so many early bears, he has no positive identifying signs but there are some clues to his date of origin – possibly just after the First World War. It is true he has glass eyes rather than boot buttons, but glass eyes were popular in England even before 1914.

He was not an expensive bear. The quality of the mohair was inferior and the pile has nearly all worn away. The ears were attached by gathering up the lower ear seam and pushing it into the head seam without requiring skilled work. To economise on fabric, the bear's legs, arms and body were cut almost straight so that there was no expensive wastage because extravagantly curved shapes had to be cut out of the fabric roll.

Bears like this were made in Britain, Japan and the United States to cash in on the popularity of teddy bears. In the United States cheap bears with similar features, which were made during the two decades following the First World War, have become known as 'Stick Bears'. Since we bought the bear in England the probability is that he was actually made in England at that time.

It is part of his charm that we shall never really know his exact origin. But one thing we can be very sure of – he was, and still is, a much-loved bear.

Vera Havers's Bear

ONE OF THE great pleasures of having a teddy-bear museum is the way in which it has introduced us to all sorts of people we would never otherwise have known. Not only do people bring their bears to look around the museum, they also send them along for holidays. One splendid summer we had a whole hug of royal bears enjoying a vacation with us, including HRH Princess Margaret's enchanting miniature bear.

As well as bringing bears to visit us, some owners donate special bears for safe-keeping. One of the first bears to join the collection was a very early British bear belonging to a lady called Vera Havers. As well as giving us the bear, Vera Havers also generously gave us a photograph of herself, as a small girl, holding that very bear. The bear, together with the photograph, now sits on a shelf in the picnic area in the company of other venerable and distinguished bears.

Having a photograph of the original owner with the bear is a great bonus for collectors and definitely increases the bear's worth, as it is valuable evidence of the bear's age and provenance, especially if it is dated. It also lends a charm that undoubtedly enhances the personality of the bear. Most important of all, it ensures that the small owner, captured at a magical moment in childhood, will always be remembered by nostalgic teddy-bear lovers.

People who collect teddy bears often like to collect artefacts of the period on which to display them. A typical example is the early perambulator shown here. Other popular items are early pushchairs, with caned backs and seats, and small period chairs. Small versions of large chairs were made by furniture manufacturers for their salesmen to take around with them as samples. One of these sample chairs makes a delightful way of displaying an old bear to best advantage.

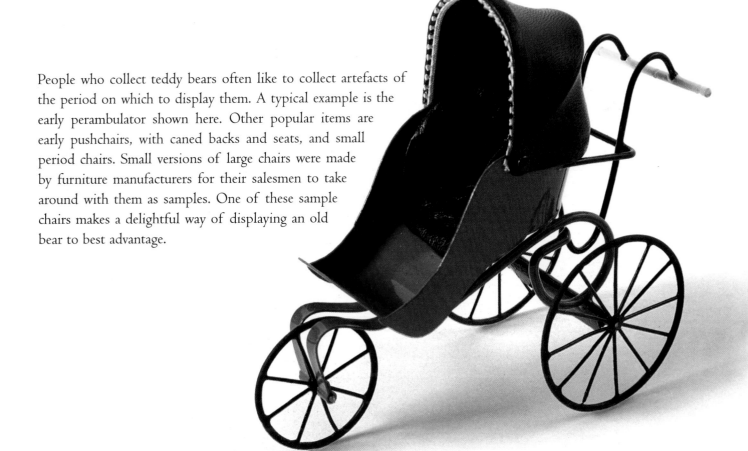

First World War Bear

THE FIRST World War was an important watershed in the history of the teddy bear. The inevitable problems of war damaged the flourishing German toy industry. Supplies of imported British mohair dried up, exports were disrupted and soft toy factories were turned over to producing goods for the war effort. Teddy-bear production in other countries was accelerated to make up for the lack of German toys. When war ended these new producers presented the German companies with formidable opposition.

Not surprisingly British teddy bears, like most aspects of life in the allied countries, reflected the spirit of patriotism. One good example was 'The Bear of Russia, Germany's Crusher', a tribute to Britain's Russian ally designed by Dean's Rag Book Company. Probably the most famous military bears were made by the Harwin Company. This firm was set up in 1914 when German bears became scarce. Dorothy (Dot) Harwin, daughter of the firm's founder, was their chief designer and her name became the firm's trademark – DOTS. Dorothy Harwin designed a series of bears, known as Ally Bears, in the various military uniforms of the allied forces. It is extremely rare to find one of these bears with its original uniform still intact after more than eighty years.

As well as buying patriotic-style bears many people dressed bears in home-made military uniform, either as presents for servicemen or to keep themselves as sentimental reminders of much-loved family members serving abroad. The bear shown here, which lives at Pollocks Toy Museum in London's Covent Garden, is a wonderful example. The bear was made in 1905 but his uniforms were made between 1914 and 1918 by a little girl called Helen Ray Lister who was seven years old when war broke out. In this picture he is wearing his policeman's outfit combined with a military hat, possibly for a stint of fire-watching.

The combination of military paraphernalia with the child-like appeal of the teddy bear makes bears like this a poignant reminder of a sad chapter in European history.

The Skier

THE GEBRÜDER BING company was already a well-established and highly regarded toy-making firm when it added teddy bears to its range early in the century. There seems little doubt that this step was a direct result of seeing the success which Steiff enjoyed with their bears. At various stages over the next three decades Bing came up against the Steiff company, which constantly challenged Bing products apparently trespassing on Steiff and their patents. Steiff may well have felt a sense of relief when Gebrüder Bing went into receivership in 1932, following the worldwide economic recession. Yet the fact that their teddy bears were made for only a comparatively short time means that early Bing bears are now as sought after as their Steiff counterparts.

The skiing bear shown here is an excellent example of one of the mechanical bears for which Bing are best known. The metal label, clearly visible on his right arm, carries the letters BW (Bing Werke) which indicates he was made from about 1919 onwards. Before the First World War the Bing trademark was a metal arrow in the ear. Following that came a label under the arm with the letters GBN (Gebrüder Bing Nürnberg) which was used until 1918.

The same basic mechanism is used for all these bears, with variations in clothing and accessories to make them appear different. A key is inserted under the left arm to wind the bear up. He then moves forward and back with the help of the walking stick attached to his right arm. As in all similar Bing mechanical bears, the left arm is straight and moves up and down. Bing mechanical bears fetch many thousands of pounds in the sale rooms, and their value is greatest when the original clothes remain intact, as in the case of this skier.

THE TEDDY BEAR HALL OF FAME

Bear-in-a-Box

I N 1917 an excited child was bought this delightful miniature bear from a six-penny stall in the Old Brompton Road, not far from Harrods. It is only 9 cm (3½ in) high but it is fully jointed. Its fur is pale gold mohair and its eyes are the smallest glass beads. To add to its undoubted charms it lives in its own elegant box, complete with leather strap.

The fact that it lives in a box is probably one of the reasons this bear has survived so well. Nowadays special bears are often supplied with a box – though rarely a leather one – and collectors are encouraged to keep the bears with the boxes to preserve their condition and their value. Obviously an original box will be invaluable later, if the bear ever comes to be sold, as a way of authenticating its origins. In the meantime it ensures that the bear is as well preserved as possible. Of course when bears were made and sold at the beginning of the century there was no thought of them ever becoming valuable antiques. They were intended for children to play with and they were expected to be handled and cuddled. Although a bear in a bad state of preservation will fetch less money than a well-preserved one, perversely some evidence that an old bear has had a loving owner will often add to its appeal.

Seventy years after it was first purchased, the miniature bear was sold by its owner and it came to live in The Teddy Bear Museum. It is always a sad moment when bears and their owners are parted, but we are sure the tiny bear feels very at home in his new surroundings and in the company of so many interesting and distinguished members of the teddy-bear family.

Rupert Bear

ON 8 NOVEMBER 1920, when *Little Lost Bear* first appeared in the *Daily Express* newspaper, no one could have predicted his enormous success. Yet in 1995 Rupert (for it was he!) celebrated his 75th Anniversary as a literary legend with a worldwide readership. The rhyming stories, set in a reassuring world where magic is always possible, have become so popular that the boy bear even has his own fan club called The Followers of Rupert.

Rupert was created by illustrator Mary Tourtel (1874–1948), who had been asked by the *Daily Express* to devise a comic-strip character to compete with the *Daily Mail*'s popular bear, Teddy Tail. When Mary Tourtel retired in 1935 the stories were taken over by Alfred Bestall. Alfred Bestall both wrote and illustrated the stories for over thirty years and added many of Rupert's best-known pals, including Tigerlily and The Old Professor.

Since Bestall's retirement in 1965 the stories have been written by a succession of writers, including Freddie Chaplain and James Henderson and illustrated by, among others, Alex Cubie. Ian Robinson is the current writer, while John Harrold draws the pictures.

When Mary Tourtel first drew Rupert he did not have his trademark outfit of red sweater and black checked, yellow trews. In those early years the predominant colour of his clothes was a pale shade of blue. At the Museum we are fortunate to have one of the very earliest Rupert storybooks, with Rupert portrayed in his original colours. Rupert stories were also included in children's annuals but it was not until 1936 that Rupert had his very own annual. A mint copy of this first annual was sold for £1,610 in 1995.

Rupert memorabilia dates from his very earliest years and Mary Tourtel's rare surviving drawings are the most eagerly sought items. Since the 1960s Rupert has been available as a soft toy. This early version, on display with other Rupert items in the Museum, is by Burbank Toys.

OPPOSITE: MARY TOURTELL, CREATOR OF RUPERT BEAR.

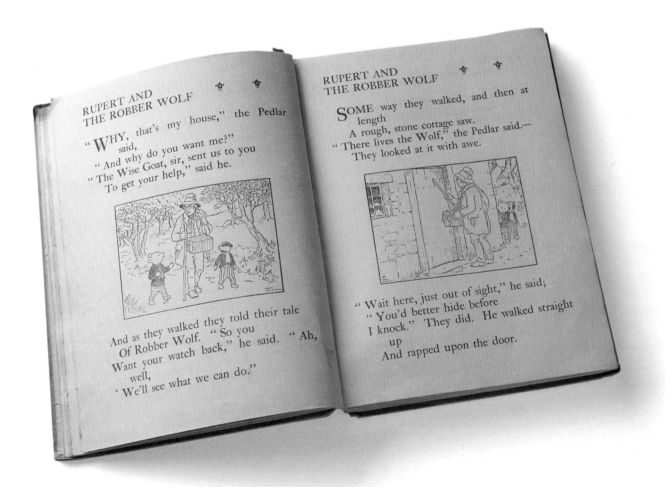

Winnie-the-Pooh

WINNIE-THE-POOH is probably the most famous literary bear in the world. Seventy years after publication of the first book in which he featured, the royalties from the books and spin-offs amount to something approaching £2,000,000 a year!

Pooh's fame rests on just three small books: *Winnie-the-Pooh* (1926), *Now We Are Six!* (1927), and *The House at Pooh Corner* (1928). Yet A. A. Milne, the writer of these classic children's stories, saw himself primarily as a serious playwright and even, on occasions, resented his success as a children's writer because he felt it distracted people from his adult work.

The teddy bear who was to become Winnie-the-Pooh was bought in 1921 for the first birthday of Milne's son, Christopher Robin, by his mother, Daphne. The bear, at first called Edward Bear or plain Bear, was an Alpha bear made by J. K. Farnell. Nowadays he lives in the New York Public Library, along with his friends Eeyore, Tigger, Kanga and Piglet, who were all donated to the children's section of the library by A. A. Milne's American publisher. Even now he is a fine specimen and photographs taken in his prime show a typically plump, glossy Alpha bear. 'He and Christopher Robin were exactly the same size on that day, ten years ago now, when the friendly bear joined the Milne family,' Daphne Milne later told an American reporter.

When he became a little older Christopher Milne decided on a more personal name for his bear. It was a combination of the name of a real bear he had admired

at London Zoo, a Canadian brown bear from Winnipeg called Winnie, and the name of a swan he used to feed in the country, which he had called Pooh. A. A. Milne explained that they took the swan's name with them when they returned to London 'as we didn't think the swan would want it any more'.

The beautiful illustrations for the books were by Ernest H. Shepard, who had already illustrated Kenneth Grahame's book, *The Wind in the Willows*. Shepard based all the characters on Christopher Milne's toys except Winnie-the-Pooh himself, who was modelled on his own son's Steiff bear called Growler.

In 1961 Walt Disney bought the film and merchandising rights to Winnie-the-Pooh and new drawings were created which gave Christopher Robin's world-famous bear a new, less sophisticated look. Disney have made several Winnie-the-Pooh films and exploited the image with great efficiency. Nowadays Shepard's original images and the new Disney images exist happily side by side.

ABOVE: A.A. MILNE, HIS SON CHRISTOPHER ROBIN, AND THE ORIGINAL WINNIE-THE-POOH.

Peter

ETER WAS MADE by a German toy firm called Gebrüder Süssenguth in 1925. His appearance is extremely fierce. He has a pointed muzzle and an open mouth, with sharp teeth and a lolling pink tongue. His eyes are made either of glass or of painted wood. When the tongue is moved from side to side a connecting lever makes the staring eyes roll from side to side.

The teddy-bear world is sharply divided about whether Peter really counts as a *teddy* bear. His realism does not tie in with the definition of a teddy bear as a doll-like version of a bear, without any of its frighteningly realistic features. Teddy-bear collector extraordinaire, Peter Bull, steadfastly refused to add a 'Peter' to his hug of bears although they shared the same name. He thought Peter was too 'menacing and aggressive' to count as a true teddy bear.

If Peter is a true teddy bear, rather than a bear toy, then the history of the teddy bear will have to be drastically rethought. This is because jointed bears, looking almost exactly like Peter, appeared in the Süssenguth catalogue in 1894, well before 1903 which is generally the accepted date for the first true teddy bear. It is also the case that Steiff showed similarly fierce fur-covered toys in their pre-1900 catalogues and many fur-covered automata were made in the nineteenth century, particularly in France.

However, the fact that not many Peter bears are found today suggests that most people felt as Peter Bull did and could not accept Peter as a teddy bear in 1925 any more than when he first appeared in 1894. This is borne out by the fact that nearly all examples of Peter are in perfect condition, not well used and loved. Most, if not all, of the Peter bears which come on to the market were found untouched and in their original boxes in an East German shop in 1974. The entire stock of one hundred was sent to England and eventually went for auction. The Peter bear shown here can be seen at Pollock's Toy Museum.

Peter certainly has a rarity value which is reflected in his sale-room price. But despite the evidence of his nineteenth-century origins he is not viewed as the descendant of the first true teddy but rather as an interesting reminder of the pre-teddy-bear age.

No/No Bear

Like so many bears this miniature bear, only 9 cm (3½ in) tall, no longer has a label. This makes positive identification and dating extremely difficult as, unless the bear has a well-documented history, it can only be done by comparing it with similar bears. He resembles miniature bears made in France in the 1920s and 1930s, the Piccolo miniature bears made by Schuco from the 1930s onwards and the Steiff miniatures made between about 1920 and 1950.

This bear's entire body, including the hands and feet, is made of the same pale gold mohair, with no paw detailing. Steiff miniatures did not have any paw detailing but during the 1920s even the tiniest Schuco bears had felt pads or paw stitching.

The fascinating detail is, of course, his double head, with one happy expression and one downcast expression. In his happy expression the little bear has an upturned muzzle reminiscent of French bears. The movement of the head is operated by a tail lever which enables it to move from side to side or to swivel in a complete circle. Steiff occasionally made bears with this circular head movement.

Unlike the famous Schuco Yes/No bears he cannot nod up and down to say 'yes' as well as 'no'. He has therefore been dubbed No/No bear.

Bear with Violin

Although they are not always soft and cuddly, mechanical teddy bears are wonderfully intriguing. This violinist, complete with miniature violin and bow, stands on little wooden feet. They do not look at all like a bear's paws but they keep his balance while he plays. He has a simple clockwork mechanism. One of the commonest problems with clockwork collectables is that the key goes missing somewhere along the way. With the violinist we were lucky that the key was still attached and that the mechanism was in working order. Old clockwork mechanisms are fragile and must not be overworked. But from time to time we take our little violinist out of his display case, wind him up and have the pleasure of showing him off to visitors as he plays his imaginary tunes.

Grandfather Bear

GRANDFATHER is the grand old man of the Museum and very much in charge. Here he is seen resting at the foot of the stairs which lead to the Hall of Fame. In this position his great size can be appreciated. He must have been a very exciting present for the small child who first owned him. Apart from an occasional wander around the Museum he lives in the oak-beamed bedroom, where many of the earliest bears can be seen. There he can usually be found, comfortably relaxed on his bed, reading his paper and surrounded by small relatives.

Grandfather bear is a most unusual Steiff bear. Made in yellow short plush, with a black stitched snout, brown and black glass eyes, and the large back hump of a traditionally styled bear, he is firmly stuffed with excelsior. As well as having the prized Steiff button still in place in his left ear, he also boasts a working growler — a rarity indeed in a bear so old. He dates from around 1920 but most of his features are those of the pre-war Steiff bears.

The year 1920 saw Steiff finally getting back to 'business as normal' after the disruptions of the First World War and the shortages in the years which followed. In 1921 the company produced a catalogue with a full range of bears in all sizes for the first time since 1914.

The beautiful plush of this giant teddy bear, who stands 117 cm (46 in) tall, contrasts strongly with the cheaper materials which Steiff experimented with in the years after the war, when mohair plush was hard to come by and prohibitively expensive. A coarse fabric, Brennessel, made from a type of nettle, was one of the alternatives used. Because supplies of mohair plush did not immediately return to pre-war levels between 1919 and 1921, the company also produced nearly 20,000 bears in paper plush made from wood pulp. Paradoxically, the bears made from these inferior fibres have become expensive collectables simply because they are so unusual.

His superb quality and distinctive size make Grandfather a perfect symbol of Steiff's determination, despite all the problems, to restore its place as the leading teddy-bear firm in the post-war years.

Schoolboy Bear

bear is a British bear which was probably made in the 1920s. He is stuffed with wood-wool and has brown glass eyes with painted black centres. His paws have been extensively worn and all four have been mended in an amateur fashion with a grey tweed fabric. Just visible beneath the mends are the remains of the original cream felt. The mohair fabric he is made of has gone completely bald, except for the area beneath the woolly jumper and blue trousers, where the original gold mohair is still recognisable. This often happens when a bear has been well used by its owner.

It is a particular problem with some of the bears made around this time by the Dean's Company, because the quality of the mohair they used was variable. The Dean's Company is the great survivor among British teddy-bear companies. Since the firm was taken over by Neil and Barbara Miller in 1988, it has concentrated on making high-quality Collectors' Bears. There is now a Dean's Collectors' Catalogue and a Dean's Collectors' Club. In the 1920s there was not the same emphasis on quality and perhaps because of this, and because they made many other animals and dolls in addition to bears, fully authenticated early Dean's bears are hard to find. In 1922 they started making bears under the A1 trademark but most surviving examples date from the 1930s onwards. With his wide-set 'mouse' ears, triangular-shaped head and cream felt pads, it is possible that Schoolboy bear is one of those elusive 1920s A1 bears.

In the case of a bear like this, where the old repairs and general wear are an intrinsic part of his charm, it would be a mistake to over-restore him. You might even take away from the value. If you do decide to repair and clean a bear in your collection, follow carefully the advice given in one of the many good books on making and repairing bears, and always be sure to retain and replace any identifying labels.

Polar Bear

THE DRINKING bear is a favourite automaton in the Museum. He is particularly unusual because he is a polar bear and is covered with white fur. There are similar bears displayed elsewhere but they tend to be covered in brown or dark brown fur.

Our polar bear was made by a French firm called Descamps. In the nineteenth century French automata were much prized for their superb quality and were very popular with collectors. This particular firm was founded in 1866 by Jean Rouellet, a Parisian toolmaker, to make mechanical toys and automata. Rouellet's daughter, Henriette, married his chief assistant Ernest Descamps and, in 1899, the firm was renamed Rouellet and Descamps. Henriette and Ernest had a son, called Gaston, who continued the firm's work until his death in 1972. The polar bear could have been made at any time from around 1890 until about 1935. Most opinion seems to favour a date of around 1930.

The bear pours liquid from a pewter flagon into his pewter goblet, then tips his head back and appears to drink it. In fact, as the cup is lifted up gravity sends the liquid back down a tube in the bear's arm. The tube runs across his back, down his right arm and back into the flagon. Our clever bear is therefore able to continue drinking from what appears to be an ever-full flagon of wine. There are many who might envy him!

As well as being able to drink, the polar bear also has a clockwork music box. So, although the open mouth and ferocious teeth make him rather fierce as a teddy bear, his many talents provide a delightfully entertaining addition to the Museum.

Yes/No Bear

THE TEDDY BEAR HALL OF FAME

T HE YES/NO BEAR was the invention of the German firm Schreyer and
Company. The company was founded in 1912 by Heinrich Müller, who
had worked for Gebrüder Bing, and Heinrich Schreyer. Initially it made
the tin and mechanical toys typical of the traditional German toy industry, but
eventually it specialised in teddy bears. Despite various changes in ownership and
a cessation of production during the Second World War, Schreyer and Company
continued creating bears until the mid 1970s. At this point, it found itself unable
to compete with the import of soft toys from the Far East and sold out to
Dundee-Combex-Marx.

Schreyer and Company was generally known by the abbreviation trademark
Schuco. In 1921 this was adopted as the official company name.

In the same year the company patented the Yes/No mechanism by which the
bear's head could be made to nod up and down or turn from left to right. To
achieve this the tail acted as a lever which was connected by a metal rod running
up through the back to the neck joint.

Yes/No bears proved to be one of the Schuco company's biggest successes and
were produced in all sorts of guises and sizes in the fifty or so years before the
company was sold. In the 1950s they were given the updated name of Tricky bears.
One of the Schuco company's most popular designs, the Bellhop bear in a smart
red jacket and pillbox hat, was produced in a Yes/No version. Yes/No Bellhop
bears fetch very high prices today.

Happy Anniversary

IN 1989 a very special bear came for a short stay at The Teddy Bear Museum *en route* for the United States. The bear had just acquired a new owner and a new name – Happy Anniversary.

Happy Anniversary was bought by American bear collector Paul Volpp as a wedding anniversary present for his wife and fellow collector, Rosemary. The present was certainly a generous one. At the time Happy Anniversary was the most expensive bear ever bought at auction, having cost an amazing £55,000 ($86,000).

Happy Anniversary is a 1926 Steiff made in dual mohair plush, a fabric which became very popular in the 1920s. New technology meant that two shades could be used to create this interesting natural fur effect. In Happy Anniversary's case, the fur is beige tipped with brown. The bear has the brown glass eyes which were also typical of Steiff bears made in the 1920s. In many respects Happy (as she is most usually known) has the features of the classic pre-war bears with a long snout and long limbs. Her face has a particularly sweet and endearing expression and she is in excellent condition but there was nothing to suggest she would achieve such a record-breaking price.

The publicity surrounding the sale, combined with the bear's undoubted attractiveness and its status as part of the Volpps' collection of over 5,000 bears, have ensured that Happy Anniversary is now one of the world's best-known bears. Her record-breaking achievement will ensure that she always maintains her value and a place in the Teddy Bear Hall of Fame.

But the last word should go to Paul Volpp who says, 'It is my wish that one beautiful little teddy bear, who caused such an international uproar – through no fault of her own – is remembered and enjoyed by all who see her as what she was intended to be, a token of my love for forty-two wonderful years with my wife, Rosemary.'

Teddy Clown

I<small>N THE</small> 1920s Steiff were busy devising novelty teddy bears to outwit the competition from companies that had sprung up outside Germany during and after the First World War. The American market was very important and Americans had a liking for dressed and novelty bears.

Teddy Clown was a perfect bear for the 'Roaring Twenties' – cute, fun and not at all serious. The bear had a pointed clown's hat with two pom-poms on the front and a ruff. The pom-poms and the edging on the ruffs were either blue or red. Very often the ruffs have not survived and have been replaced with bows.

Thirty thousand Teddy Clowns were produced between 1926 and 1928. They had the kapok stuffing and glass eyes which were typical of the 1920s. Many of them, including the extra large 115 cm (46 in) version, were made in the tipped mohair plush (dual plush) so popular in the 1920s. This fabric was very luxurious and made a welcome change after the economy fabrics of the early post-war years. Teddy Clown was also made in pink or gold plush in the smaller sizes only. On a few of these bears the small red label attached under the ear button, which replaced the white label in 1925 and which was used until 1935, can still be found.

Several replicas have been made of this attractive bear including a Limited Edition of 10,000 in 1986, two versions of Teddy Clown Junior for the United States in 1987 and 1989, a replica of the 1928 Teddy Clown as a Steiff Club Edition in 1993–4 and a Miniature 16.5 cm (6½ in) Teddy Clown in white, pink or gold in 1993 as part of the Historical Miniatures series.

Original versions of Teddy Clown fetch at least £3,000 in the sale rooms and the replicas have also become expensive collectors' items.

Schuco Perfume Bottle Miniature

THE MANAGER of the Museum, Sylvia Coote, is the lucky owner of this attractive novelty bear. It is typical of the miniature bears made by the German company Schuco in the 1930s. The bear itself is approximately 9 cm (3½ in) high. It has jointed limbs and is made from clipped gold mohair stretched over a metal frame. The fact that there are no clearly defined paws indicates that the bear could not have been made in the 1920s, when Piccolo Schuco bears had little feet and front paws made of felt.

The delight of this bear is the fact that there is a glass perfume phial, complete with original glass stopper, concealed inside the body. Similar bears were made with powder compacts and lipsticks hidden inside. They were intended to be used on dressing tables or even to be popped into handbags. This particular bear is in wonderful condition and was probably never used to store perfume but left on display and appreciated purely for its decorative qualities.

Bear and Monkey

T HERE ARE very few animals in the Museum other than the teddy bears for which it was created, although if you look carefully in the bedroom you might spot a pair of audacious mice peeping up through the old oak floorboards. The bedroom also houses the only other interloper – a dark brown monkey. He is there as one half of a Schuco automaton, together with a very attractive teddy bear. The bear has large, flat oval feet typical of 1930s Schuco bears. Because it was never possible to pick it up and cuddle it, it is in absolutely immaculate condition.

The automaton was made in Germany in about 1935. Since Schuco was founded by a former employee of Gebrüder Bing, who specialised in mechanical toys, it is not surprising that this company also concentrated on novelty and mechanical bears of very high quality.

Unlike the other mechanical bears in the Museum, which are clockwork driven, this one is electrically operated. Both animals have brown and black glass eyes and rather fetching 1930s-style spectacles. The teddy moves his head from side to side, as if reading a newspaper, while the monkey nods his head approvingly. When the pair arrived in the Museum it was clear that they should have something to read. There was no clue to their original reading matter so a suitably dated copy of the *Radio Times* was provided for them.

Merrythought M Bears

THE TEDDY BEAR HALL OF FAME

MERRYTHOUGHT began manufacturing teddy bears and other soft toys in September 1930. The company was originally founded in 1919 in Yorkshire, to weave mohair yarn, but the recession threatened trade and a soft-toy outlet seemed an innovative way to use the fabric which was being made. The mill owner, W. G. Holmes, persuaded A. C. Janisch, who worked for Farnell, and C. J. Rendle, who worked for Chad Valley, to help him set up his new company. They found premises in Coalbrookdale, Shropshire. Although the little town is now called Ironbridge, Merrythought still operate from their original site.

Merrythought were lucky to find an exceptionally gifted designer in Florence Atwood, a deaf and dumb girl and schoolfriend of C. J. Rendle's daughter, who stayed with the firm until her death in 1939. In 1931 they produced their first catalogue which featured the Magnet bear. In the catalogue the letter M was used to indicate the bear was made of mohair. Next to the Magnet bear in the catalogue stands a bear called the Merrythought bear made from the same pattern, but more expensive because he was made out of the newly fashionable fabric art-silk plush. In the catalogue he is denoted by the letter S.

The name Magnet was dropped almost immediately. In the 1932 catalogue exactly the same photographs of the Magnet bear were used but this time he too was called a Merrythought bear. Collectors often use the term 'M bears' for all early Merrythought bears made from the original pattern, probably on the assumption that M stands for Magnet or Merrythought. In fact the actual catalogue letter changed with the type of fabric used. Merrythought themselves still refer to this original pattern, used for the first Magnet bears, as the M pattern, and many of the bears they make today are based on it.

Both the label and the button on these handsome bears, made in the early 1930s, feature the Merrythought trademark, a wishbone. 'Merrythought' is an old English word for a wishbone and the company's intention was to make children's wishes come true. It has been achieving this aim without interruption ever since 1930. Even more unusually, Merrythought remains a family firm, and the current managing director, Oliver Holmes, is the grandson of the founder.

Musical Bears

THE TEDDY BEAR HALL OF FAME

MUSICAL BEARS are a particularly pleasing species of novelty bear. They are a natural development from the musical boxes and automata of the eighteenth and nineteenth centuries and the tradition of mechanical toys that had grown up in Germany in particular.

The musical boxes inserted in early bears were usually Swiss in origin, the Swiss being world famous for the quality of their clockwork mechanisms. The musical boxes were activated in different ways, either the straightforward key-wind method or a starter which worked by pressing or squeezing the bear's back or tummy to release a coiled spring. Steiff made musical bears using a Swiss-made version of the squeeze-operated mechanism. A strategically placed label carried the words 'Squeeze me gently here, then you music hear'! J. K. Farnell produced a range of musical bears in the late 1930s which featured an exclusive musical movement by the Swiss company, Thorens. Nowadays music boxes often originate in the Far East, where they can be made more cheaply. Although clockwork mechanisms are the traditional way of achieving a musical bear there are more modern alternatives, such as audio cassettes.

The bear pictured here is one of several musical bears who live in the Museum, some of which can walk and sing at the same time. He was made some time in the 1920s and is an unusual style, with a comparatively small head and body combined with very long straight arms and legs. He is made of pale gold mohair with black shoe-button eyes. He has his original fawn-coloured felt pads and clear black-claw stitching. The musical element is an old-fashioned wind-up musical box which plays a traditional tune.

Since singing is so good a thing,
I wish all bears would learn to sing.

William Bearyd, 1588

If music be the food of love, play on...

Duke Ursino in William Shakesbeare's *Twelfth Night*

There's music in all things, if bears had ears.

Lord Bearyon

Music is well said to be the speech of angels.

Thomas Carlyle Bear

Come, let's away to prison;
We two alone will sing like birds in the cage.

William Shakesbeare, *King Bear*

Music has charms to sooth a savage breast.

William Congreve Bear, *The Mourning Bride*

Pooh had once invented a song which went:
Tra-la-la, tra-la-la,
Tra-la-la, tra-la-la,
Rum-tum-tum-tiddle-um.

A. A. Milne

The Prince of Love

I N   A   S U R V E Y among visitors to the Museum this bear was voted the bear most like its owner. He belongs to the romantic novelist Dame Barbara Cartland, who specialises in historical romances about beautiful, innocent heroines and dashing, rakish heroes.

Since she published her first novel at the age of twenty-one Dame Barbara has featured for many years in *The Guinness Book of Records* as one of the world's all-time top-selling authors, with titles such as *Bitter Winds of Love*, *Wings on My Heart* and *The Viscount's Revenge*. In 1984 she received La Médaille de Vermeil de la Ville de Paris for selling over 25,000,000 books in France alone. For the last eighteen years she has written an average of twenty-three books a year. Versions in more than twenty-seven languages have sent her total sales to over 600,000,000 books.

The Prince of Love, as Dame Barbara named him, epitomises the teddy-bear version of her romantic heroes – a very Rudolph Valentino of a bear. He is gorgeously arrayed in an assortment of jewels. Around his neck is a bow in the shade of deep pink which has become Dame Barbara's signature colour. Note too his unusual cupped ears, set low down on the side of his head, and the painted eyes which have quite a twinkle to them. In giving him to the Museum, Dame Barbara provided us with those life-enhancing elements of glamour and romance which brighten up the dullest day.

Accompanying this literary bear is a little handwritten poem:

> *I am a special Teddy Bear*
> *I am very particular what I wear.*
> *My diamonds gleam like the stars above*
> *As really I am The Prince of Love.*

Purse Bear

Teddy-bear novelties swiftly followed the invention of the teddy bear. Indeed the first advertisements for teddy bears, way back in 1906, were not for teddy-bear toys but for teddy-bear sidelamps for motor cars.

Since then the imagination and ingenuity applied to adapting and exploiting the teddy bear for as many uses as possible have been phenomenal. One of the most popular adaptations has been to turn teddies into bags and purses.

The teddy-bear purse shown here is made of blonde mohair plush, has jointed limbs, brown and black glass eyes, a stitched snout, felt pads and wood-wool stuffing. Without a doubt this is not simply an unusual purse but a true teddy bear.

Unlike many teddy-bear novelty items, purses tend to get put to practical use. The worn fabric on this purse shows it was well-used by its owner. Purses are still a popular teddy-bear item although they tend to be shoulder purses, with a teddy-bear face and zip fastener, rather than the type of metal-framed snap-fastening purse shown here. This style of purse is not fashionable today but it was a type that was common in the first fifty years of the century. Given the traditional style and without any label to identify the teddy-bear manufacturer, experts have differed on the origin of this teddy-bear purse, giving dates as far apart as 1910 and 1940.

The Skater

A T THE END of the 1930s a novelty bear started to appear in the Chiltern catalogue. He was a teddy-bear skater, 38 cm (15 in) tall, made from gold artificial silk plush, which was a popular fabric during the inter-war period. Chiltern produced their first art-silk bear, known as Silky bear, in 1929.

Integral with the bear is a blue mohair plush jacket with a white collar. On the bear's head is a matching pillbox hat. These bears were also made with pink jackets, presumably to make a pair of a boy and a girl. Sadly this skater bear has lost the little white mohair muff he originally carried. As well as being dressed in an interesting way, the bear also has a characterful face. His nose is prominent and has the black vertical stitching used on all Chiltern bears.

Skater bears were made by Chiltern until the mid 1950s. We are very fortunate to have one of these attractive and highly collectable bears at The Teddy Bear Museum.

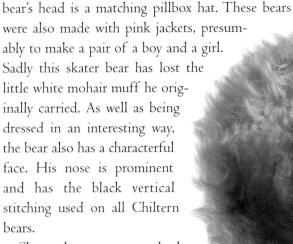

Ragged

D URING THE Second World War, when fabric was scarce, knitted and crocheted teddy bears became quite common. Women's magazines printed patterns for them so that children would not be deprived of the comforting presence of a teddy bear. Discarded sweaters were unravelled, and the wool re-used, to make up the teddy-bear patterns. Nowadays old hand-knitted bears, each one unique, but once thought of as second-best to the real thing, are eagerly snapped up when they come on sale.

The bear shown here is not one of those wartime teddies exactly, but a close relation. He was once, as his short arms indicate, a very typical British bear from between the wars. He belongs to the actor Richard Briers, and beneath the woolly suit is a bear which was so enthusiastically loved by him and his sister that he would fall apart without the protection it gives.

A label, written by Richard Briers and attached to the bear, tells the story:

This was my teddy, but when my sister lost her panda on Wimbledon Common (which broke her heart) I gave it to her. Many years later she gave it back to me to give to my younger daughter. By then he was very ragged. So my mother crocheted his outfit to hold him together, and my daughter gave him the name 'Ragged'.

THE TEDDY BEAR HALL OF FAME

Theodore

THEODORE IS A tiny bear with a big reputation. He was Peter Bull's favourite bear and travelled everywhere with him in his pocket. Peter and Theodore were together for more than thirty-five years. They both loved foreign travel and Peter gave Theodore a miniature Anglo-Greek dictionary to help him on their many trips to the Greek island where he had a small house.

'I have to insure Aloysius for vast sums when he goes out on modelling jobs without me. And yet, in my heart of hearts, Theodore is far more valuable to me. I still regard him as my Best Bear Friend,' Peter Bull once wrote.

Theodore is a gold plush miniature Steiff bear, just 9 cm (3½ in) tall. He was given to actor and arctophile Peter Bull as a first-night present by his friend and fellow actor, Maurice Kaufmann. Peter Bull was interested in astrology and the astrological chart drawn up for Theodore gives his exact birthday as 28 April 1948.

As he revealed in his best-selling book, *Bear With Me*, Peter Bull's much-loved childhood teddy bear had been given to a jumble sale by his mother while he was away at boarding school. As Peter recalled, 'This made me sit and sulk throughout the holidays, fiercely resenting the fact that this cherished symbol of security had been so thoughtlessly discarded.'

It was Peter Bull's unashamed love of Theodore (he once called Theodore 'a symbol of unloneliness'), together with his readiness to talk about him and the rest of his growing collection of bears, which helped unlock the floodgates of nostalgia that fuelled the teddy-bear craze of the late twentieth century. Theodore is therefore a Very Important Bear in teddy-bear history. On 11 December 1995, Theodore was sold at auction for £14,625, a very large sum for a very small bear.

Chad Valley Bear

THE CHAD VALLEY company took its name from the location of its first premises. Like many British firms they began making bears in 1915, when supplies from Germany were interrupted.

This Chad Valley bear is a splendid example of one of the company's most popular styles which was made, with minor variations, from the 1930s through until the 1960s. He is fully jointed, made of mohair and has the typical large ears set wide apart on the head. The shaved or clipped muzzle is a feature of these Chad Valley bears, as is the prominent nose. Only the bears made at the beginning of the 1930s have a more triangular, stitched nose. Also a feature are the large oval feet, usually stiffened with a layer of card.

Several clues are available to help date these bears reasonably accurately. For example, the earliest bears had paws made of traditional felt. At the end of the 1930s an artificial leather, Rexine, became the popular choice for paws. Our bear has dark brown velvet paws, which were common in the 1950s and 1960s. Perhaps most significant is the Royal Warrant label attached to the foot. Chad Valley bears were bought by HM Queen Elizabeth for her daughters, the Princesses Elizabeth and Margaret. In 1938 she granted the firm her Royal Warrant, which was shown on a woven label stitched to the foot of all Chad Valley bears from 1938 onwards. On the death of George VI, Queen Elizabeth became Queen Elizabeth the Queen Mother and the Chad Valley Royal Warrant changed accordingly. Our bear has a label saying 'By Appointment Toymakers to HM Queen Elizabeth the Queen Mother', so we know he was made after the 1953 Coronation.

Chad Valley bears of all styles were extremely popular and sold in large numbers. They were of excellent quality so they have lasted well. This means they are relatively easy to find now, and make a good area to specialise in when starting a collection.

Baby Book

Our bookworm bear hails all the way from Japan. After the Second World War Japan led the field in mechanical toys, operated by clockwork or batteries. The studious little bear shown here (he is only 17.5 cm/7 in tall) dates from around 1950 and is very typical of his period and origins. The fact that the book is an alphabet book in English indicates clearly that he was made for export. He is constructed with a moulded tin frame (the feet are painted tin) on to which are glued red overalls and a head and body covering of brown nylon plush. The bear is wound up with a key in the back and the right arm moves up and down. A magnet on the right hand attracts the tiny pages of the book and flips them over so that the bear appears to be reading.

Japan has had a thriving toy industry throughout the twentieth century, most of it aimed at the cheaper end of the market. Recently it has also begun to play a new role in the creation of high-quality, traditional and handmade bears. While continuing to be involved in the mass market, at the other end of the scale it is also becoming known for bear artists, like Kazuko Ichikawa and Kazuyo Kindo, who create enchanting and very individual bears.

Jackie Baby

I n 1953 Steiff celebrated the Golden Jubilee of the teddy bear with a Jubilee bear called Jackie Baby which, like Teddy Baby introduced in 1929, was described as 'a comical young bear cub'. This Jubilee bear was produced from 1953–5.

Jackie was designed to be more of a cuddly soft toy than the traditional Steiff bears it celebrated. The Steiff company was well aware of the fact that fashions in teddy bears were changing and that the soft-toy animals being imported from the Far East were eroding their market share. In celebrating the past they took the opportunity to look to the future and to introduce some radical new ideas.

Although Jackie retained the longish snout of classic Steiff bears, the overall style was innovative. The differences are immediately apparent when the new bear is placed next to one of his predecessors. The hump was dropped, so Jackie Baby has a straight back. The legs are extremely short and chunky, with large, squared-off paws. Jackie Baby's legs are jointed, although many of the other new bears introduced at about this time, such as Soft Bear, had movable arms only. The arms themselves are disproportionately long and the paws are straight, not spoon-shaped at all. This bear has an extremely round, fat body

which, because of the short legs, is very low-slung. Combined with his large, round head, it accentuates the fact that he is a roly-poly cub and not a grown teddy bear.

Two features particular to Jackie Baby are the dark 'navel' in the middle of the bear's tummy and the pink stitch sewn horizontally across his vertically stitched brown nose. In his left ear he has the new (1952) Steiff button with the name Steiff embossed in cursive script. Sewn into a side seam on the body is an extra label with the words 'Made in US-Zone Germany', which was used on Steiff toys from 1947–53.

Following on from this Jubilee bear, Steiff produced a number of soft-toy bears such as Cosy Teddy. One of the most successful was the Zotty (shaggy) bear, with its long soft fur and open mouth, which is still produced today. In 1966 Steiff altered its basic bear pattern yet again, having changed it in 1950 for the first time since 1905. The 1966 revised bear, which remained the standard design until 1993, shared many features introduced with Jackie Baby, including the short legs and round, baby-shaped body with no hump.

Jackie Baby was produced in a fine mohair plush in four sizes, 17 cm (7 in), 25 cm (10 in), 35 cm (14 in) and 70 cm (28 in). The largest and the smallest are shown here together. As part of their programme of issuing replicas of previous successes, Steiff made Jackie Baby replicas in 1987, 1988 and 1989. In 1990 an edition in pink mohair, called Jackie Bear Rose, was issued in the USA.

Wendy Boston Playsafe Bear

THE WENDY BOSTON Playsafe Bear was one of the most distinctive styles to evolve after the Second World War. It was the invention of Wendy Boston, a Londoner who began making bears as a hobby and then set up her business in South Wales.

Between 1954 and 1976, when the firm finally closed, there were many different colours and sizes in the Playsafe range. All have the same, distinctive, Wendy Boston look epitomised by the 1960s example pictured here, which is on loan to the Museum from actress Bonnie Langford.

Wendy Boston Playsafe bears are made from manmade fibre and are unjointed. Their short arms and legs are cut in one piece and are permanently outstretched, as if waiting for a cuddle. The ears are cut in one piece with the rest of the head and the muzzle is large and round.

This distinctive style grew from the fact that they were designed to be safe, machine-washable and very cuddly. In 1954 Wendy Boston test-marketed the first fully washable teddy bear, with nylon plush, foam stuffing and securely fastened eyes.

In the 1960s, at the peak of its success, Wendy Boston Playsafe Toys was responsible for making more than a quarter of Britain's soft-toy exports.

Ice-cream Bears

THIS PAIR OF clockwork bears repeatedly raise their ice-creams to their lips, while slowly revolving on the spot. They are made from tin with a covering of acrylic plush. Their googly eyes and their open mouths, with tongues ready to lick their ice-creams, give them rather sweet expressions. They came with a Schuco key but their appearance is more consistent with the Russian, or Eastern European, mechanical toys of the 1950s.

Clockwork mechanical bears like these may appear primitive in the light of what can be achieved with modern technology. But their old-fashioned simplicity is an essential part of their charm and they appeal to collectors now that battery-operated and electronic toys have become the norm.

Balalaika Bear

IN THE NINETEENTH century the Eastern European countries, like their neighbour, Germany, had a thriving toy industry. After the Second World War, toy making continued as one of the area's industries, despite the trading problems which resulted from the East-West divide. Czechoslovakia and Romania, among others, produced mechanical tin toys very much like those that had been made at the beginning of the century when the Germany company Bing led the field. On display in the Museum is a typical painted-tin, clockwork carousel, with four bears seated in swing chairs, which revolves like a ferris wheel. It was made in Romania in the early 1960s.

This charming mechanical bear could hardly display his origins more obviously. He is playing the traditional Russian stringed instrument, the balalaika, which resembles a guitar but has a triangular body. He was made in Russia in the mid 1950s. Russia, where bears still roam wild, has a tradition of making bear toys and this is a good example. He is just under 25 cm (10 in) tall and made of tin, covered with brown felt. Still having the original box contributed significantly to his value.

Mr Whoppit

B ASED ON A character from the *Robin* comic, this unusual little bear was made by Merrythought in the mid 1950s. He has an unjointed all-in-one body, blue felt feet, a black-stitched nose and mouth and large, pointed ears lined with blue felt.

Mr Whoppit was given to land-and-water-speed record holder Donald Campbell in 1957, as a lucky mascot, by Campbell's engineer, Peter Barker. Donald Campbell named the bear Mr Woppit (the spelling later changed with the addition of an 'h'). A small blue-bird was embroidered on the bear's jacket because Donald Campbell always named his speed machines *Bluebird*.

Mr Whoppit was with Donald Campbell when he broke the world land-speed record at 403.1 mph in 1964 and on the seven occasions he broke the world water-speed record. He was with him on the day of *Bluebird*'s fatal crash on Lake Coniston in January 1967. Because of his light, kapok stuffing, Mr Whoppit floated to the surface and was retrieved. He went on to be the mascot for Donald Campbell's daughter, Gina, when she made her own record-breaking attempts at the women's world speed records. On these later occasions he prudently wore his own little life-jacket.

Mr Whoppit does not have a classic bear's good looks but his unique history lifts him out of the ordinary. In recognition of this, Merrythought made a replica of Mr Whoppit in 1992.

Paddington

THE BEAR WHICH was to become Paddington was bought by Michael Bond as a Christmas present for his wife in 1956. He caught sight of it, sitting on a shelf in Selfridges department store in London, and felt he could not leave it alone over Christmas. His good deed has been rewarded many times over because the lonely little bear inspired the Paddington stories which have conquered the world and changed the entire direction of Michael Bond's working life.

Michael Bond and his wife named the new bear Paddington, after the large London railway terminus near their home. The first story, *A Bear Called Paddington*, describing Paddington's arrival from 'darkest Peru', was written by Michael in only ten days, and published in 1958.

In 1972 the first Paddington soft toys were produced by the British company Gabrielle Designs, owned by Gabrielle Clarkson. Gabrielle Designs gave Paddington the wellingtons which have since become another of his trademarks, along with eating marmalade sandwiches. Their purpose was purely practical, so that the toy bear could stand steadily on his feet and look like the bear in the original illustrations by Peggy Fortnum. They were such a success that wellingtons are now an integral part of Paddington's character and he is always drawn with them.

In 1975, the US licence was transferred to the American company Eden Toys while Gabrielle Designs continue to hold the UK licence. The modern Paddington seen here is a British bear made by Gabrielle Designs, which also make versions of Paddington's Aunt Lucy from Peru.

Paddington has put his great success to good use by lending his name to The Paddington Club, for supporters of the medical research charity Action Research. Money is raised through Paddington-shaped collection boxes and through activities organised by the club for this worthwhile cause.

THIS LITTLE Paddington, sitting comfortably in his armchair, was used for the very first series of Paddington animated films. These were five minutes long and made for television using the stop-go animation technique. The furniture surrounding Paddington comes from the same series, which was made by the British film company, Filmfair. After the series was completed the company destroyed most of the props, but Michael Bond managed to rescue Paddington and one or two of his most personal bits and pieces. He generously donated them for display at the Museum.

In recognition of his worldwide fame, his charity work and his generosity, Paddington was presented with a Teddy Bear Museum Lifetime Achievement Award in 1996. The following response was received from his West London address: 'Everyone at number thirty-two Windsor Gardens was suitably impressed to hear about Paddington's Lifetime Achievement Award, and postcards are winging their way to the Home for Retired Bears in Lima.'

Aunt Lucy must indeed be proud of her nephew and all he has achieved since he set out on his great adventure nearly forty years ago.

A legend is born when a very small bear from Peru finds himself at the very large London railway station from which he takes his new name — Paddington.

Tru-to-Life

THIS BLACK BEAR, sometimes called a grizzly bear in catalogues, is one in the Tru-to-Life series, which was made by Dean's in the mid to late 1950s. The first in the series was a white polar bear. Polar bears became fashionable after a baby polar bear was born at London Zoo in 1949. The Tru-to-

Life bears were designed by Sylvia Wilgoss, who joined the company in 1952 and became their chief designer in 1956.

A Tru-to-Life bear is extremely unusual precisely because it *is* so realistic. The unique charm of teddy bears is often said to be the fact that they lack the ferocious appearance of the real thing, so this style is something of a daring departure from the standard teddy.

The bear is unjointed and is extremely floppy as the arms and body are only lightly stuffed with a mixture of kapok and wood-wool. To give the bear its authentic sitting posture the legs are more firmly stuffed, with wood-wool only, and sewn on to the front of the body, rather than directly underneath.

The rather frightening appearance of the face and claws is achieved by moulding them from flesh-coloured rubber. Black mohair, like that used for the body, is then stretched over the rubber face mask, allowing the muzzle and nose to protrude through. The muzzle is covered in white acrylic mohair but the extremely realistic black rubber nose is left uncovered. This particular bear still has a working tilt growler, so he is able to sound as ferocious as he looks.

Hugmee Bear

CHILTERN BEARS were one of the most highly regarded British bear manufacturers. Their greatest success were their soft, kapok-filled Hugmee bears, which have a distinctive posture because the soft-filled bodies do not adequately support their large heads. Hugmee bears were first advertised in 1923 and were made until Chiltern were taken over by Chad Valley in 1967. In over forty years they went through quite a few changes.

In the 1920s and 1930s Chiltern Hugmee bears had large bodies and long arms. The legs had very fat thighs and narrow ankles. Feet were a large, flat oval shape and made of velveteen reinforced with card. The bears had protruding, shaved muzzles and their noses were vertically stitched with a distinctive raised stitch at either end. Eyes were of clear glass and made secure with an extra stitch at the back of the head. These features, combined with good-quality mohair, created a very generous style of bear.

The economies of production necessitated by the Second World War radically altered the appearance of Hugmee bears. Their bodies became smaller, the arms were much shorter, the nose stitching lost the raised stitches and the feet became smaller and tear-shaped. Because the bodies were smaller the heads looked larger in proportion. To save on materials, the face became flatter and the dropped head became even more noticeable.

Chiltern bears did not carry sewn-in labels until the 1940s and the cardboard chest labels have almost invariably been lost. This bear does not have a sewn-in label but he is clearly one of the later Hugmee bears. The reddish-brown glass eyes and velveteen paws were used both during and after the war but this particular bear's realistic moulded plastic nose, first used in 1958, identifies him as a typical 1960s Hugmee bear.

Sooty is an impertinent little glove puppet who enjoys dousing his audience with a water pistol. He has been a regular performer on British television since 1952, a feat that has earned him a place in *The Guinness Book of Records*.

The very first Sooty glove puppet was bought by Harry Corbett in 1948, while he was on a works outing with his family in Blackpool. Similar glove puppets were marketed by more than one firm at this time and we do not know who made it. Harry Corbett added character to the standard puppet by rubbing his ears and nose with soot from the chimney. So at the same time the bear acquired a unique appearance and a memorable name. Harry, an amateur magician who dreamed of becoming a professional, was looking for an interesting gimmick to add to his act. But, as he himself later said, 'The teddy quickly became the star and I was relegated to the role of his assistant.'

Harry's son, Matthew, took over the Sooty Show when his father retired, and has been equally successful. Over the years, Harry, and later Matthew, have used dozens of Sootys because of the inevitable wear and tear of showbusiness. The Sooty who lives in the Museum is one of the earliest. He belongs to disc jockey Mike Read, who bought him at a charity auction. Look closely and you can see the glue on his paws which was used to keep his magic wand in place.

Once television had made Sooty a star, special Sooty puppets quickly went on sale. Chad Valley made puppets like this one from 1952 until 1980 and they make a delightful addition to any collection — just watch out for the water pistol!

Cheeky Bears

IN THEIR 1957 catalogue Merrythought introduced a new registered teddy-bear design which was to prove one of their most consistently popular characters. His name was Cheeky. In the words of the catalogue he was 'The new bear of irresistible charm'.

A Cheeky bear is easily recognisable. He has a domed head and low-set, cup-shaped ears with trademark bells sandwiched inside the layers of cloth. His muzzle is shaved or made of a separate fabric such as velvet, with the fabric gathered into the nose. Perhaps most important of all is his broad smile, created with wide stitches curving out from the nose.

Since his very first appearance, when he was pictured striding jauntily across the page, Cheeky has been a bear who prefers to walk rather than sit. His striding posture is an integral part of his character. Cheeky shares a lot of the features of the Punkinhead bear (although not its punk-style quiff of white mohair!) which was made by Merrythought in 1949 as a special order for a Canadian department store.

Since 1957 Cheekys have been produced in innumerable sizes, colours and varieties, including the pink and blue nylon fabric popular in the 1950s and 1960s. As well as appearing as a traditional teddy bear, Cheeky has also been seen as a Guardsman, a Clown and a Beefeater, to name but a few. There have also been many Cheeky novelty items such as purses, muffs, nightdress cases, and a Cheeky carousel.

The Cheekys in the Museum include two very early versions in artificial silk plush and a 1960s example in gold mohair.

Original Nisbet Bear

THE HOUSE OF NISBET, one of Britain's most influential teddy-bear manufacturers, began life in 1953 as Peggy Nisbet Ltd. Peggy Nisbet made collectors' dolls and later, when the company had become famous for teddy bears, it still continued making the dolls for which it had built up such a reputation.

Jack Wilson, a Canadian, joined the company in 1975 to help run it on behalf of one of its major investors. Under his chairmanship the company changed its name, in 1976, to The House of Nisbet, and added teddy bears to its range. The very first teddy bears were designed by Peggy Nisbet's daughter, Alison.

When The Teddy Bear Museum opened in 1988, Jack Wilson was immensely encouraging and supportive. To include in our display he gave us an Original Nisbet Bear, which he and his family brought when they came to Stratford-upon-Avon to visit the newly opened Museum. Jack Wilson and Alison Nisbet had married, making The House of Nisbet a family firm once more. Their son William was born in 1978 and was ten when he came with his father to the Museum.

The bear is extra special because it is William Nisbet's own bear. The written description accompanying the bear states: 'This is the original Nisbet Teddy Bear, promoted by William Nisbet Wilson in his first year in 1978. Donated by William, Boxing Day 1988.'

Like all House of Nisbet bears, this is a classic design and set the tone for all their later bears. He is made of dense gold mohair, has two-tone, wide-set, brown glass eyes, a brown stitched nose and velvet pads. He stands 30.5 cm (12 in) tall and is fully jointed. Being a young bear he wears a bib with The House of Nisbet logo embroidered on it. The printed label, which the bear is reading, has a picture of a baby and the words 'This is my Nisbet teddy bear. He is a good bear and he loves me.'

Fozzie Bear

SOME BEARS are natural stars and Fozzie bear is one of them. He lives in the Hall of Fame and is one of the original puppets made by the late Jim Henson for his pioneering television programme *The Muppet Show*. He is made of acrylic plush and the wide-set ears, with a battered old hat placed between them, the dotty pink and white neckerchief, the red nose and googly eyes all contribute to his unique and lovable character. Fozzie is a failed comedian, who is constantly being thwarted as he tries to tell his stories. It is his constant good humour in the face of obstacles, and his readiness to bounce back after repeated failure, which endear him to his audience. In many ways he is like the music-hall stars of yesteryear, who trod the boards around the time the first teddy bear made his appearance.

Fozzie has his place in this book as the representative of a whole group of bears who have made their names through the media, like the Care Bears and Super Ted. They include Baloo the Bear, the lovable bear based on Kipling's character in *The Jungle Book* who was brilliantly brought to life by the Disney cartoon studios and the voice of Phil Harris. Their big advantage is that, unlike traditional toy bears, they have the power of speech to express their personalities.

We can expect more such larger-than-life showbiz bears in the future.

Meanwhile, lights, camera, action
. . . and:

It's time to put on make-up
It's time to dress up right
It's time to get things
started on The
Muppet Show
tonight!

Smokey Bear

Smokey Bear is the symbol and mascot of the US Cooperative Forest Fire Prevention Campaign. His image is familiar all over the United States. He was adopted as the Fire Prevention Mascot in 1944, when forest fires were becoming more frequent as people increasingly used forest areas for recreational activities. At first he appeared on posters and in promotional literature looking very like one of the real brown bears which roamed wild in forest areas.

Over the years his earlier, natural image evolved into the dressed teddy bear Smokey of today. His jeans, or dungarees, and hat are based on the clothes of a real-life forest ranger.

All sorts of Smokey novelty items have been produced over the years in all the guises that might be expected – postcards, books, ashtrays, figurines, plates and mugs. So much was made that a law had to be passed saying that only the Department of Forestry was authorised to exploit the Smokey image. Early Smokey memorabilia is now a great favourite with collectors.

Much of the promotional material now being tracked down by collectors was originally designed with children in mind, to remind them of the importance of fire safety. Chief among them are Smokey teddy bears which are bought by adults as often as children.

The first company commissioned to make Smokey Bears was the Ideal Company. A conventional soft-toy version was made in 1953. A year later a version of Smokey bear with a vinyl face, hands and feet replaced it. Ideal created a number of bears with this new feature in the early 1950s and the new Smokey fitted in with the pattern. In the 1960s, Ideal changed the style to a conventional fabric bear in brown artificial plush, with a yellow muzzle and hands, and a protruding tongue. During the 1960s and 1970s the Knickerbocker Toy Company made their own versions of Smokey Bear and recently other American firms have produced versions, including Dakin Inc.

The Smokey Bear in the Museum was made by Three Bears Inc. of Newport, Rhode Island in 1989, and was donated by writers Ken Thomson and Charles Osborne.

Bully Bears

PETER BULL was undoubtedly one of the most influential figures in the Great Teddy Bear Revival. He was the spokesman for all the adults of his generation who secretly retained an affection for the teddy bears of their childhood and who wanted to keep alive the tradition of classic teddy bears. By talking on television about his own hug of bears, and by writing his own history of teddy bears, he helped to turn the tide in the 1960s and 1970s, when it looked as though the true teddy bear might become simply another cuddly soft toy.

In 1979 Jack Wilson, director of The House of Nisbet and himself a key player in the Teddy Bear Revival, asked Peter Bull to apply his knowledge and love of bears to designing a new bear, incorporating all the best qualities of the old-fashioned, classic bears. The result was the family of Bully bears, named as a tribute to Peter Bull himself.

Peter Bull's other interest, apart from teddy bears, was astrology. These two interests met when he and Jack Wilson continued their fruitful partnership with the Zodiac bears series, based on the twelve signs of the zodiac.

On the sofa are four prized Bully bears from the Museum collection, with a selection of Peter Bull memorabilia including a Limited Edition of his book, signed by the great man himself. From left to right are a Limited Edition Captain Bully, a Bully in a Woolly Pully with embroidered mottoes reflecting Peter Bull's sense of humour (they include 'Save water, bath in Retsina' and 'Life is a cucumber'), a Limited Edition classic Bully complete with waistcoat and bow tie, and a Limited Edition Bully Minor.

Sir Jasper

S IR JASPER is one of a very small Limited Edition by Norfolk bear artist Pamela Johnson. He is one of the Museum's largest bears, about 122 cm (48 in) tall, and he usually sits on a chair in the library. Because of his size Sir Jasper is always asked to dress up in a red Father Christmas outfit and play Santa at Christmas. One of his pleasantest duties is to hand over a small present from his sack to the mayor of Stratford-upon-Avon who, by tradition, comes to switch on the Museum's Christmas lights.

Pamela Johnson's bears, which go by the name of Bunbury Bears, were sold in aid of Good Bears of the World, the charity set up by Jim Ownby to give teddies to children (and adults) in hospital.

The signed labels which accompany Bunbury Bears state: 'This is a Bunbury Bear. He is made for you, entirely by hand, by Pamela Johnson. His aim in life is to make you happy. He will share your joys and sorrows, receive your confidences, and never tell tales, and he will give you undying love.' Hardly surprising then that their coat of arms is a bear and a pot of honey, with the motto *Ursus Semper Fidelis* (The Ever-Faithful Bear).

Teddy Ruxpin

W HEN TEDDY-BEAR collectors think of mechanical bears they usually think in terms of wind-up clockwork mechanisms or early automata. While these reflect the nostalgic appeal of teddy bears, there are also more modern forms of mechanical bear.

This 1988 version of Teddy Ruxpin, created by the large American toy firm Mattel, who also make the Barbie doll, is a good example. His mechanism is not designed to make him move but to make him talk. In some ways it might be considered a more up-to-date version of the growler. A battery-operated audio cassette inside the bear's body tells stories. This unusual feature makes Teddy Ruxpin an ideal bear to leave in the room with a small child who wants company before drifting off to sleep.

William Shakesbeare

AT HIS DESK in the library, scribbling away with a goose quill pen, sits the true William Shakesbeare. Unlike Winnie-the-Pooh, who was frequently referred to as a bear of very little brain, this is a bear of very great brain indeed. Among his finest plays are *Macbear*, *The Merry Bears of Windsor* and *Two Gentlebears of Verona*. His best-known poem begins with the memorable line, 'Let me not to the marriage of true bears admit impediment.'

Although undoubtedly the greatest writer the teddy-bear world has ever known, he likes to take inspiration from the works of the other great authors whose works and portraits grace the library. These include George Bearnard Shaw, and the authors of such classics as *The Hunchbear of Notre Dame*, *The Encyclopaedia Beartannica* and *Bearchester Towers*.

William Shakesbeare was designed and made in 1988 by Jack Wilson, of The House of Nisbet, and Gyles Brandreth. He is a fully jointed bear, 56 cm (22 in) tall and made of a fawn artificial plush. His eyes are of brown and black glass and his paws are brown velvet. His most notable feature is his high forehead, based on the only known portrait of William Shakespeare and similar to his appearance on the Shakespeare Memorial at Holy Trinity Church, Stratford-upon-Avon. To achieve this authentic look, the bear's face and muzzle are made of a fawn, tweed-type fabric which complements the colour of the fur. William Shakesbeare wears a plain white linen collar and a red-lined black Elizabethan cape. Only one of these bears was made. Like the original Bard of Avon, the Bear of Avon is unique!

Steiff Shakesbeare

Unlike his Nisbet counterpart, the Steiff William Shakesbeare bear is in no way intended to be a representation of his famous namesake. He was created in honour of the great Stratfordian and as a tribute to him. The bear is, in fact, a replica of a 1909 Stieff. He is about 28 cm (11 in) tall, fully jointed and made from gold mohair. A similar small bear was used to make the first Steiff stringed-puppet teddy bear (Pantom Bär).

Bears in this style were also used as table gifts at a Gala Banquet in New York on 6 June 1910 to welcome back President Roosevelt after the two-year-long vacation in Africa and Europe which followed his retirement from office. The little bears were dressed in safari suits based on those worn by the president while hunting in Africa. It may be that the gifts given at this dinner gave rise to the apocryphal story that the teddy bear got its name from similarly dressed Steiff

bears used as table gifts at the wedding, some years earlier, of Theodore Roosevelt's daughter. Alice Roosevelt categorically denied having any sort of teddy bears at her wedding breakfast but the story has been repeated over the years despite her denial.

William Shakesbeare is typical of the Steiff Special Editions which have been issued since 1980 and which are almost invariably based on replicas of earlier favourites. The William Shakesbeare Special Edition was limited to 2,000 pieces available only from The Teddy Bear Museum. For technical reasons Steiff has found itself unable to complete the edition, which means that the William Shakesbeares already in circulation will have an unforeseen additional rarity value.

Gyles Bear

Gyles Bear is a Signature Edition limited to 5,000. He is 38 cm (15 in) tall, made of gold mohair and is fully jointed with a small hump to his back. The signature which each bear carries is that of Gyles Brandreth, co-founder of The Teddy Bear Museum. The bear was the idea of Jack Wilson and was designed by Gyles and The House of Nisbet in 1989.

In 1989 Gyles was working on a number of television programmes and had become known for wearing colourful jumpers. Most of these jumpers were designed by George Hostler, a knitwear designer and lecturer in design at De Montfort University. George's exclusive designs were popular with a number of people, including Elton John and the Princess of Wales. When Gyles Bear was being designed it was clear that the bear could not be fobbed off with any old jumper. So George Hostler was asked to design a jumper exclusively for the teddy bear.

In 1989 Jack Wilson relinquished control of The House of Nisbet to the American company Dakin and moved to California. After some confusion, production of The House of Nisbet collectors' bears and dolls passed to the Welsh company Diane Jones International. It continues to make Gyles Bear and other high-quality bears under The House of Nisbet name. All of these, including Gyles Bear, carry The House of Nisbet label stitched to the left foot.

Vampire and Devil

GAIL EVERETT is a creative bear artist who designed a number of bears for us when the Museum first opened. Gail pioneered what might be called 'the alternative bear'. A favourite theme in the late 1980s were her 'punk' bears. These are thoroughly traditional bears with the surprising additions of studded leather jackets and quiffs of brightly coloured hair. There are two of Gail's original punk bears relaxing on deckchairs in the Teddy Bears' Picnic. This is an area of the Museum where bears by many of Britain's leading contemporary bear makers are on display, with bears by, among others, Susan and David Rixon of Nonsuch, David Wright, and Sue Quinn of Dormouse Designs. There are also bears by Glenn and Irene Jackman who, as Hugglets, have had such a success with their magazine and the *Hugglets UK Teddy Bear Guide*.

Gail created her one-off Dracula and Red Devil bears, especially for the Museum, to celebrate Hallowe'en 1988. Inspired by being told that her bears were 'out of this world' she went away and came back with two bears which really do conjure up worlds not usually associated with teddy bears. Fortunately, both Dracula, with his fangs and red satin-lined opera cloak, and the Red Devil, with his tail and toasting fork, seem more impudent than wicked. They always cause amusement when visitors catch sight of them, lurking up in the rafters.

Marmaduke

MARMADUKE IS THE Museum Bear and is a very worthy holder of the title. He is based on the Museum's logo, an unashamedly old-fashioned classic bear in the tradition of the very first teddy bears. Marmaduke was drawn for us by artist and designer, Michael Buckner. When we saw him we realised that he needed a seriously old-fashioned name to match his appearance and Marmaduke immediately sprang to mind. Marmaduke is extremely gratified by the fact that in the United States his name is usually shortened to Duke.

In 1989 The Teddy Bear Museum was honoured with an award from the British Tourist Authority. To celebrate we decided to create our first ever exclusive Limited Edition, and to base it on the bear which symbolises the Museum around the world. We decided to limit the edition to 1,988 to mark the year in which the Museum opened.

Marmaduke was designed by Valerie Lyle of Big Softies. He is 46 cm (18 in) tall, fully jointed and handmade from gold mohair. He has black glass eyes and his paws are light brown suede. Big Softies was established by Valerie and her husband Fred in 1978. This Yorkshire-based family firm specialised in making very large animals and they were the people who had made the giant teddy bear (some 3 m/10 ft tall) which sits near the entrance to the Museum. This enormous bear makes a wonderfully cosy seat for small children who love to sit on the bear's legs and play with the smaller teddy bears which surround him.

In 1996 Big Softies was taken over by another well-known British teddy-bear company, Gabrielle Designs, who will continue to make the Marmaduke Limited Edition.

Jubilee Bear

THE JUBILEE BEAR was created in 1990 by Merrythought to celebrate their Diamond Jubilee. It was a totally new teddy-bear design by chief designer Jackie Revitt, whose teddy-bear designs have ensured that Merrythought teddy bears remain at the forefront of the collectors' market. Jackie, who joined the firm in 1971, designs a whole range of animals for Merrythought, but bears are a favourite: 'To be able to make a new bear is absolute heaven.'

Jubilee Bear was made in a Limited Edition of 2,500. He was made in 45.5 cm (18 in) size only, out of pale gold mohair with matching maize-coloured pads. He is a very traditional bear, with a broad face and cup-shaped ears on the side of his head. His body is stuffed with polyester, but the muzzle is stuffed with wood-wool to provide a firm base for the hand-stitched nose. The Union Jack label stitched to the right foot was woven specially for this particular bear and was not used on any other Merrythought bear. At the centre of the Union Jack is a diamond with the dates 1930–1990. The front-opening box used for Jubilee Bear was a new concept in teddy-bear boxing and one which has become popular since it first appeared.

Following on from the success of their Jubilee Bear, Merrythought issued a bear for their 65th Anniversary in 1995. Called Blue Sapphire Bear, it was a small blue bear, designed by Jackie Revitt, and presented in a sapphire-coloured box.

The King and Queen of America

THE UNITED STATES pioneered the concept of artists' bears. At the beginning of the 1970s, when most of the world was still in the teddy-bear doldrums and Peter Bull's pioneering book, *Bear With Me*, had not long been published, a small number of creative people were making individual artists' bears on the west coast of the United States. As the teddy-bear revival slowly gathered pace, the number of bear artists increased and there are now bear artists working all over the world, including Japan.

However, the United States is still the main centre for gifted bear artists creating unusual and characterful bears. No collection would be truly complete without examples of their work. This delightful pair of Jubilee Bears was created for the Kansas City 1990 Teddy Bear Jubilee by bear artist Monty Sours of Gladstone, Missouri, and her husband Joe. They were donated to The Teddy Bear Museum by Bill Boyd, host of the Kansas City Teddy Bear Jubilee and a well-known figure in the teddy-bear world.

Little Red Bear

Naomi Laight is a prize-winning British bear artist. She has been interested in expressing her creativity through sewing since she was a child. The first bear she ever made, which still lives with her, was created from her grandmother's cape and given the name 'Hessel'.

After making bears for the children in her own family she began selling them in small numbers. Encouraged by her success, she started experimenting with different methods of doll-making and for a period concentrated on making handmade dressed wax dolls in authentic period styles.

When she eventually returned to making teddy bears her experience with antique-style dolls was evident in the traditional styling of the bears. Many of the bears she makes are re-creations of the earliest bears and she frequently uses distressed mohair and black eyes to reinforce the effect.

Although Little Red Bear is not in a traditional colour he displays many of the features of Naomi Laight's very recognisable creations. His nose is vertically stitched in the classic fashion, he has light-coloured suede pads and clearly stitched black claws. His eyes are not glass but flat black plastic, which gives the same look as the boot-button eyes of the earliest pre-1920 bears. The traditional look is underlined by the long arms and slender tapering feet.

Naomi Laight makes individual bears and very small Limited Editions. She has also designed larger Limited Editions for the Dean's Rag Book Company. The Teddy Bear Museum is proud to include her Little Red Bear as part of its extensive collection of British artists' bears.

Wellington

WELLINGTON WAS designed to a completely new pattern especially for the launch of Merrythought's first Collectors' Catalogue in 1991. Wellington came in two sizes, 38 cm (15 in) and 53 cm (21 in), and production was limited to 2,500 for each size. His fur is the nostalgic, bronzey shade of gold which was very popular immediately after the war.

Wellington has two noticeable features. He was the first Merrythought bear with such a pronounced muzzle, a style detail which they have repeated from time to time since. In addition he was made in an innovative whirled mohair fabric, which gives him a particularly interesting texture.

Merrythought's first Limited Edition Collectors' Bear appeared in 1981. This bear, the E (for Edwardian) bear was highly traditional in style and was made for the American market only. Merrythought have continued to create teddy bears exclusively for the American market. Typical examples are the Micro-Cheekys, including a Mountie and a Forty-Niner (based on the early American gold prospectors) which were produced in 1995.

In the early 1980s, the United States was still the only country where arctophilia had become a recognised pastime and teddy-bear collecting was taken really seriously. By 1991, when the Merrythought Collectors' Catalogue was launched and Wellington was designed, teddy-bear collecting had also become established in Britain and Europe and was beginning to grow into a significant pastime worldwide.

Humphrey Beargart and Lauren Bearcall

HUMPHREY BEARGART and Lauren Bearcall are two of the Museum's starriest bears. They were inspired by the legendary screen partnership of Humphrey Bogart and Lauren Bacall and combine the nostalgia of the teddy bear with the romance of the greatest years of the cinema. Lauren Bearcall's glamorous image is underlined by the fact that she is made of a red man-made fabric with a silky sheen to it and wears a full-length fake fur coat and a 1940s-style hat with a fetching little veil. Humphrey Beargart sports the raincoat and slouch felt hat worn by the film star in so many of his best-known roles.

Both these delightful bears are Limited Editions made by the prestigious American teddy-bear manufacturer, The North American Bear Company. This company was begun by Barbara Isenberg in 1978 and is based in Chicago. One of the company's most successful bears, introduced in their launch year, was Albert the Running Bear, who became the hero of a popular series of children's books.

Humphrey Beargart and Lauren Bearcall are two of the characters from The North American Bear Company's Very Important Bear Series. This series of Limited Editions was launched in 1980 to create bears based on celebrities from the worlds of entertainment and literature. A key feature is that the names always feature a play on words to include the word 'bear'. It also makes great use of the company's speciality of creating beautiful clothes and accessories for their bears. When Humphrey Beargart and Lauren Bearcall arrived at the Museum in 1989 they brought a touch of Hollywood to Stratford-upon-Avon.

I'm Henry VIII, I Am!

FROM TIME TO TIME The Teddy Bear Museum commissions its own greatly prized Limited Editions. Because of the Museum's historic connections it was decided to create a unique bear to mark the 500th anniversary of the birth of one of Britain's best-known monarchs, Henry VIII. His Ursine Majesty Henry VIII Bear was enthroned in the Tudor Hall of Fame at noon on 28 June 1991, exactly 500 years to the day after the birth of his namesake, Bluff King Hal.

This roguish bear, with a distinct twinkle in his eye, is inspired by the Holbein portrait of the monarch who is best remembered for his six wives. He was specially created for the Museum by the Welsh bear artist Sue Schoen, whose enchanting handmade bears are collected by bear lovers around the world. Sue Schoen's company is called Bocs Teganau, which is Welsh for Toy Box, and its bears are represented in the Museum by the miniature family of Mami Siân, Dadi Dylan, and their children Gareth, Catrin and Baby Rhian, who live in the Victorian dolls' house.

Henry VIII Bear was made in a Limited Edition of 200 only. He stands 29 cm (11½ in) tall, is fully jointed, made from gold mohair and wears a lined velvet cape and a bead-encrusted feathered cap. On his arrival at the Museum he was introduced to William Shakesbeare and was most gratified to find that the great dramatist had written a play based on his very eventful life.

M.K.K. Bear and Phoebe

EVERY COLLECTOR has a favourite bear. Peter Bull's was Theodore, Colonel Bob Henderson's was Teddy Girl and ours is M.K.K. Bear. Like Teddy Girl she is unusual because she is quite definitely female, while most teddy bears remain resolutely male. Her crisp little broderie anglaise dress, with its pale pink ribbon, and the bonnet, set at a jaunty angle, show off the character of her face beautifully and evoke the spirit of a bygone age. M.K.K. Bear's origins cannot be verified but she certainly has all the characteristics of a Georgian bear from the period 1910 to 1936 when George V was King of England. Her eyes are glass, she is jointed, with a small hump and her snout is quite pronounced, with a nose of vertical black wool stitching. Interestingly, the pads on her hands and feet are scarcely indicated and are made from the same beige plush as the rest of the body.

Because M.K.K. Bear is such a special bear she usually lives at home with us. Recently she has been on an extended stay at the Museum. During the visit she has been enjoying the companionship of Phoebe, her replica, seen here seated in front. Phoebe was made exclusively for The Teddy Bear Museum in a Limited Edition of 200 by the Dean's Company and shares all M.K.K. Bear's endearing characteristics. One of these exclusive bears will remain permanently in the Museum as part of the display when M.K.K. Bear eventually returns.

The Teddy Bear Museum

STRATFORD-UPON-AVON

THE GRAND OPENING IN STRATFORD-UPON-AVON, JULY 1988.
THE MAYOR AND MAYORESS ARE SURROUNDED BY ALL THE PEOPLE WHO
HELPED TO CREATE THE TEDDY BEAR MUSEUM.

When my husband Gyles and I had the idea of starting a Teddy Bear Museum we did not fully realise that we were part of a growing trend — what has been called Bear Awareness. Looking back, we now realise that by founding the Museum we were a small part of the snowballing enthusiasm for teddies which had gathered pace since Peter Bull published *Bear With Me* in 1969.

My first teddy bear was given to me as a student — a twenty-first birthday present from a friend. Gyles's bear consciousness stretches back much further. As a child, he owned a much-loved bear by the name of Growler. Sadly Growler went absent without leave one day and has yet to return. Clearly a substitute had to be found. So, in the carefree days before we had children of our own, we began to collect old and interesting teddy bears while foraging around junk shops and

4 July 1988, Independence Day, the American Ambassador, the Hon. Charles H. Price II, with a guardsman bear and two small teddy bear enthusiasts.

market stalls. Teddy bears had not then become such (dare I say it?) over-priced collectors' items. Each new bear was a pleasure and not an overly expensive pleasure. As the collection grew we occasionally wondered where it would end. When we bought a house in Stratford-upon-Avon the answer became apparent. What could be more satisfying than to create a permanent home of their own for our bears in that historic market town?

This exciting project finally came to fruition on 4 July 1988 when The Teddy Bear Museum was launched by the then American ambassador to London, the Hon. Charles H. Price II.

We had chosen 4 July, American Independence Day, as our tribute to the fact that the Teddy Bear owes its name to the 26th President of the United States, Theodore Roosevelt.

BELOW: THE BEDROOM IN THE MUSEUM. THIS ROOM IS FULL OF ENCHANTING EARLY BEARS MADE DURING THE FIRST HALF OF THE CENTURY.

The ambassador joined in the festivities in Regent's Park, London, just a short walk from his official residence, with great good humour, despite being almost overwhelmed by crowds of young admirers and their bears.

At the height of the celebrations a small bear was launched by balloon, carrying a message of goodwill to whoever found him. He was cheered on his way in the general direction of Stratford-upon-Avon. Sadly, no one has ever been in touch to say that they found him at his final landing place. Even so we have still not completely given up hope that one day, after many thrilling adventures, he may find his way home to the Museum.

Following this launch, the Museum was officially opened by the Mayor and Mayoress of Stratford-upon-Avon, Councillor Dr Geoffrey Lees and Mrs Lees. Our sense of becoming an integral part of Stratford was enhanced by the fact that, prior to becoming the Museum, 19 Greenhill Street had been for many years the home of Archer and Coote, jewellers and watchmakers, and Sylvia Coote joined us as manager of the Museum.

Also among the many people who celebrated the opening were Sarah Tisdall, the designer responsible for the wonderfully witty murals which bring the Museum to life; Sergio Ransford, the architect who so sympathetically turned the 400-year-old building into a suitable home for so many hundreds of bears; and Stefan Bednarczyk, who arranged and performed the teddy-bear music.

Since 1988 it has given us enormous pleasure to see The Teddy Bear Museum become a popular destination for visitors to Stratford-upon-Avon and a magnet for teddy-bear lovers from all over the world. The collection has grown, not just because we have been unable to resist new additions but because bears are sent to us by their owners for holidays and long stays. The late Marquess of Bath sent his bear Percy to live with us permanently, but insisted on covering the bear's ears while we discussed details of his journey, as Percy had been told he was coming for just a short break!

A few years later Raymond Seitz succeeded Charles Price as American ambassador to London and his wife Caroline kept up the connection by sending her own teddy bear to the Museum for a summer holiday. He arrived with a suitcase sensibly packed with pyjamas, toothbrush, toothpaste, a hairbrush and, most thoughtfully of all, his own miniature bear to cuddle up to at night.

All our visitors, human and ursine, are greatly welcome. They bring the Museum to life and give it its unique character. As the twentieth century draws to a close we celebrate the worldwide success of the Teddy Bear and look forward eagerly to what will be achieved in the next one hundred years.

It would be impossible to list all the teddy-bear shops, or even all the teddy-bear collections and museums, which have sprung up over the last few years. Listed below are a few of the better known and longest established ones. The best way to find out about shops, museums, bear artists, teddy-bear fairs and much, much more is to buy one of the excellent teddy-bear magazines now being published. By reading them you will quickly familiarise yourself with all the most up-to-date news of what is happening in the world of teddy-bear enthusiasts.

Directory

MAGAZINES

United Kingdom

Hugglets Teddy Bear Magazine
Hugglets UK Teddy Bear Guide
(British Teddy Bear Association)
PO Box 290
Brighton BN2 1DR

Teddy Bear Scene
7 Ferringham Lane
Ferring
West Sussex BN12 5ND

Teddy Bear Times
(The British Bear Club)
Avalon Court
Star Road
Partridge Green
West Sussex RH13 8RY

United States of America

Teddy Bear and Friends
Cowles Magazines Inc.
6405 Flank Drive
Harrisburg
PA 17112

The Teddy Bear Review
PO Box 1239
Hanover
PA 17331

Teddy Bear Times
3150 State Line Road
Cincinnati
North Bend
OH 450052

Japan

Teddy Bear Post
Japan Teddy Bear Fan Club
2–3 Nangu-Cho
Ashiya City
Hyogo 659

MUSEUMS

United Kingdom

The Bear Museum
38 Dragon Street
Petersfield
Hampshire GU31 4JJ

Bethnal Green Museum of
Childhood
Cambridge Heath Road
London E2 9PA

The London Toy and Model Museum
21–3 Craven Hill
London W2 3EN

Museum of Childhood
42 High Street
Edinburgh EH1 1TG

The Teddy Bear Museum
19 Greenhill Street
Stratford-upon-Avon
Warwickshire CV37 6LF

Teddy Melrose
The High Street
Melrose
Roxburghshire TD6 9PA

The Wareham Bears
18 Church Street
Wareham
Dorset BH20 4NF

MUSEUMS *(continued)*

Germany

Steiff (Margarete) Museum
Alleenstrasse 2
Postfach 1560
D-7928 Giengen (Brenz)

United States of America

The Carrousel Shop and Museum
505 West Broad Street
Chesaning
MI 48616

Teddy Bear Museum of Naples
2511 Pine Ridge Road
Naples
FL 33942

SHOPS AND COLLECTORS' CLUBS

United Kingdom

Asquiths' Teddy Bear Shop
10 George V Place
Thames Avenue
Windsor
Berkshire SL4 1QP

The Dean's Collectors Club
The Dean's Rag Book Company Ltd
Pontypool
Gwent NP4 6YY

Merrythought International
Collectors' Club
Ironbridge
Telford
Shropshire TF8 7NJ

Sue Pearson Antique and
Collectors' Bears
13½ Prince Albert Street
The Lanes
Brighton
East Sussex BN1 1HE

Teddy Bears of Witney
99 High Street
Witney
Oxfordshire OX8 6LY

United States of America

Bears N Things
14191 Bacon Road
Albion
NY 14411

The Calico Teddy
22 East 24th Street
Baltimore
MD 21218

Index

INDEX